*Trans*formational
DIVERSITY

*Trans*formational
DIVERSITY

....

WHY AND HOW INTERCULTURAL COMPETENCIES CAN HELP ORGANIZATIONS TO SURVIVE AND THRIVE

Fiona Citkin
Lynda Spielman

Society for Human Resource Management
Alexandria, Virginia
www.shrm.org

Strategic Human Resource Management India
Mumbai, India
www.shrmindia.org

Society for Human Resource Management
Haidian District Beijing, China
www.shrm.org/cn

The Society for Human Resource Management (SHRM) is the world's largest association devoted to human resource management. Representing more than 250,000 members in over 140 countries, the Society serves the needs of HR professionals and advances the interests of the HR profession. Founded in 1948, SHRM has more than 575 affiliated chapters within the United States and subsidiary offices in China and India. Visit SHRM Online at www.shrm.org.

Interior Design: Blair Wright
Cover Design: Blair Wright

Library of Congress Cataloging-in-Publication Data
Citkin, Fiona.
Transformational diversity : why and how intercultural competencies can help organizations to survive and thrive / by Fiona Citkin and Lynda Spielman.
    p. cm.
Includes bibliographical references and index.
ISBN 978-1-58644-230-9
1. Management--Sociological aspects. 2. Management--Cross-cultural studies. 3. Cultural pluralism. I. Spielman, Lynda. II. Title.
HD30.19.C58 2011
658.30089--dc22
                    2011014392

11-0125

Contents

"The dogmas of the quiet past are inadequate to the stormy present. The occasion is piled high with difficulty, and we must rise with the occasion. As our case is new, so we must think anew and act anew."

— Abraham Lincoln

Chapter 1. Reaching Our Potential with Transformational Diversity

The latest research in diversity, *Global Diversity and Inclusion: Perceptions, Practices and Attitudes,* commissioned from the Economist Intelligence Unit by the Society for Human Resource Management (SHRM),[1] points out that although North America ranks high for diversity, the potential is far from fulfilled, with the region scoring only 70 out of 100 points. The need to reach our potential is more challenging in our uncertain times. At the same time, organizations need to grow and remain competitive, more so now than ever before. This reality is why the business rationale for transforming diversity and inclusion that we advocate and substantiate in this book rests with synergy-boosting intercultural training for everyone.

In this book we introduce Transformational Diversity© — a new vision of diversity developments that seeks to revise and transform current diversity programs through a strong infusion of an intercultural perspective with intercultural business competencies training. This new brand of diversity is taking the "old" diversity beyond race and gender, proposing the shift of focus from traditional race-gender to minorities-integration-synergy-performance issues. The shift — which we believe to be of special significance in the time of economic challenges and rapidly changing demographics — needs special attention: women, as well as U.S.-Americans of color, are regarded as easier to integrate into corporate cultures (for they share the prevailing national cultural norms), while other ethnic minorities and overseas employees may present more complex issues of cultural backgrounds and styles of thought. Many business professionals already understand that different demographic groups think and communicate differently, and these cultural differences need to be understood by all stakeholders — so that the newcomers to the workplace can be integrated sooner rather than later. Integration is not easy to achieve, but the expectant prize of an enhanced bottom line resulting from an inclusive, harmonious, and collegial organizational culture is well worth the effort.

The necessity to complement traditional diversity efforts with consistent, frequent intercultural training that regards national culture as a key differentiator is validated in the above-mentioned research. The aforementioned SHRM research report states:

> "As organizations recognize the importance of developing greater cross-cultural competence, diversity and inclusion practitioners are often at the forefront of this work. This makes sense, as these professionals have long been engaged in helping individuals in ways that allow people from all backgrounds to hear and be heard, understand and be understood, and work together productively. And some will suggest that one's national culture is the most powerful differentiator there is, greater than ethnicity, gender or language."[2]

This thought has been convincingly outlined in recent intercultural research, such as *The Cultural Imperative* by Richard Lewis, who explains how some cultural traits are too deeply ingrained to be homogenized.[3] Also worth remembering is that presently many established concepts and approaches are becoming outdated and therefore require considerable modifications to survive and thrive. Transformational

Diversity, a diversity practice imbued with solid intercultural business competencies training, is inclusive by its nature, and it embraces some best "old" diversity practices (like compliance, affinity groups, and such), but it moves them off center stage as things once necessary but insufficient in today's organizations. It is Transformational Diversity that the nation embattled by change needs.

BACKGROUND

The concept of Transformational Diversity was developed in response to broadly expressed client needs for moving forward while making diversity work more effectively to enhance productivity and performance. The diversity function or discipline of human resources focuses on employee differences as expressed by their experiences, backgrounds, personal qualities, and work style orientations, such as race, age, ethnicity, and disability that can be recognized and used for an organization's business objectives. Inclusion, on the other hand, recognizes that the presence of diversity alone is not a guarantee of success and represents commitment and actionable steps to achieve business benefits; primary among these is a corporate culture that makes people feel respected and welcome.[4] The coupling of inclusion-as-action with diversity developments has been brewing for years,[5] but now more than ever, diversity should contribute more visibly to productivity and the bottom line to justify its investment. In other words, diversity should change to achieve its full potential.

Transformational Diversity was designed for an increasingly multicultural workplace, which we characterize as the presence and interaction of groups of people of different national and ethnic backgrounds to include their linguistic, socioeconomic, and religious characteristics. In this regard, Transformational Diversity serves as a large umbrella for North American diversity with international interests. It offers powerful potential not only for global but also for pre-global organizations. Transformational Diversity is about a new diversity imperative that transcends traditional diversity and inclusion programming by placing inclusion in the driver's seat. This is the essence of Transformational

Diversity. We offer strategic and tactical resources for seamlessly bridging the current diversity-inclusion gap and for making diversity globally prepared — within the context of dramatically changing demographics and increasingly multicultural human capital that is in need of appropriate talent development initiatives.

GOALS

We wrote this book with several goals in mind.

First, it will help HR and diversity leaders who may need to reenergize or revisit their work, as we will explain, in light of pressures from increasingly diverse workforce populations to develop globally minded corporate cultures during challenging economic times. We will discuss the main purpose of examining human capital's intercultural competencies initially in Chapter 2 and more substantially in Chapters 3, 4, and 5. This book was written to deliver a call to action in response to domestic diversity practitioners who are struggling to reawaken their efforts in more meaningful directions.

Second, we intended to write the book not only for the "best in class for diversity" companies but for all organizations, big and small, where HR professionals and business leaders are concerned with workforce talent development and productivity. We offer new and different strategies and plans that deal with what is not working in many current diversity programs and what is needed now. The book tackles, foremost, the complex issues of cultural diversity for the benefit of employee engagement.

Finally, we believe that diversity today, to a considerable degree, boils down to its ability to support the organization's ultimate goals of growth and productivity (that is, profitability, market share, innovation, and more) and needs to embrace intercultural understanding of both global and local human capital to achieve those goals. The new incarnation of diversity that we present in this book is pragmatic, practical, and productive — and also entertaining and exciting with its connection to people's interests in their own professional growth and in putting a new set of skills to work for the good of their organizations. We think of Transformational Diversity as a diversity renaissance totally in sync with modern times.

Chapter 2. The *Essence* of Transformational Diversity

This chapter will describe the fundamentals of the Transformational Diversity approach and how it compares with the "old" diversity practices.

We begin with the definition of Transformational Diversity and outline the vision leading to distinguishing diversity from inclusion. Next we explain our concept and innovation recognizing the current reality in which "old" diversity challenges abound, while multiculturalism and inclusion issues are often ignored, no matter how detrimental this action may be to the health of an organization's culture. We also advocate today's diversity value proposition by briefly introducing the new diversity imperative that accepts Transformational Diversity as effective in confronting the multicultural issues in organizations today.

DEFINITION

Transformational Diversity is a call for change in current diversity and inclusion programs, which in our experience seems to be struggling from fatigue and from challenges to produce measurable results. Transformational Diversity incorporates and infuses a cross-cultural perspective with intercultural business competencies training. This vision represents a change that can produce a practical, tangible effect on the bottom line, as we will show, and makes Transformational Diversity a rainmaker, or a high achiever, as opposed to typical stagnating "domestic" diversity that is often challenged to contribute to improving the companies' financial realities. Transformational Diversity focuses on leadership and a workplace culture that are inclusive and also relevant to the organization and to its business objectives.

CONCEPT AND INNOVATION IN A NUTSHELL

Designed for the reality of an increasingly multicultural and global workplace, Transformational Diversity aligns with the new imperative to focus on inclusion as defined by practice over the past few years as company after company seems to have changed its "diversity" initiatives to "diversity and inclusion." The "new imperatives" for further diversity developments (addressed in detail in Chapter 3) include the need to compete worldwide for the best talent, which is usually more attracted to companies known for having inclusive cultures; the need to develop global workforce initiatives; the need to coordinate all domestic efforts with an increasingly multicultural workforce; the need to have diversity contribute more visibly to performance and the bottom line; and the need to organize inclusion-oriented systematic education for *all* populations. These new imperatives have been duly taken into consideration and embedded in our Transformational Diversity vision and practices that describe intercultural awareness and skill-building and that apply them to everyone in the organization — which is why Transformational Diversity is a natural fit with a focus on inclusion. More specifically, Transformational Diversity also offers a challenge to "old diversity," which is alive and well — presenting a revised value proposition for diversity work and a new imperative for action.

DIVERSITY IS THE STATE OF MIND
WHILE INCLUSION IS ACTION

We believe that organizations and the general population have a general awareness of the concept of diversity. However, the inclusion capability (the goal of diversity) is often limited, with the grip of prejudice — or unconscious bias — still too tight, even for some highly educated people in both corporate and social/political arenas. Some social pundits would argue we are tired of diversity, and others, including legislators, are more direct in limiting their tolerances to certain groups, such as immigrants. As we write, the current downturn in the economy has led to greater job layoffs and a politicization of views as to how to move toward national economic health. In this regard, immigrants especially seem to be the target of local prejudice as more people vie for fewer jobs. There exists a broad, self-sufficient value assumption that if we have freedom from prejudice, everyone will be able to contribute to the best of one's ability, and then the overall results — including bottom-line results — will improve. This assumption value tells us loudly and clearly: we need to considerably extend current diversity efforts on behalf of inclusion to become a truly democratic society, with freedoms that include freedom from prejudice and freedom from unconscious bias.

Example. A diversity director based in the New York area recently shared this story with us:

> Whatever we do — and you know how big we are with diversity numbers and women issues — we seem to be unable to eradicate some built-in intolerances . . . Just the other day my own assistant who is retiring told me that she and her husband decided to retire to [X] "because there are no foreigners." Clearly, in this woman's mind, [the] northeastern U.S. has too many "foreigners." Perhaps, too, as a diversity practitioner she had reached the point of diversity "overload."

(Of course, plenty of Mexican Americans and Central and South American immigrants live in the southeast and southwest United

States, so assuming she meant "foreigners" to mean these populations, her premise was as flawed factually as it was prejudicial.)

The point. If a diversity professional exposes deep social intolerance of "foreigners" — read as "anybody different from me" — in her mind and in her life, diversity is not connected with inclusion. Therefore, the "old" or traditional diversity achievements of the company failed with respect to its major goal, that is, to instill inclusion as social acceptance of diversity of minds and appearances. To achieve this goal, we must dig more deeply so that we can move from diversity as a *state of mind,* which is passive, to inclusion as *action,* a topic on which we will elaborate in Chapter 3 and also identify through specific training and development programs in Chapter 5. The objective is not for individuals to want to "run away" to avoid living near or working with certain groups, as was the case with the above-mentioned employee, but rather to acquire — through training — skills to work on one's own personal attitude toward inclusion and to take steps for actively "running toward," that is, coming to like, if not enjoy, a more tolerant environment and a more tolerant self. This solution is one way to appreciate the real positive contributions that inclusion can make in our lives.

Thus, the essence of Transformational Diversity is characterized by vision, strategies, and tactical applications for seamlessly bridging the current diversity-inclusion gap within the context of today's workforce, characterized by growing numbers of women, immigrants, and older employees. As the source of labor force data, the U.S. Bureau of Labor Statistics reports that the current rate of participation by women in the U.S. workforce at 47 percent is significantly higher than it was in the 1970s. What is most notable in recent years is that more employed women have children and are working full time and year round than in the past decades. More specifically, the proportion of women with a college degree has tripled over three decades.[1]

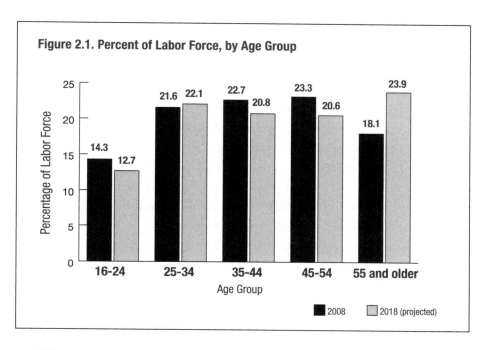

Figure 2.1. Percent of Labor Force, by Age Group

With regard to the aging of our workforce, the projections offered in Figure 2.1 for both men and women indicates that by 2018, employees of age 55 years or older will likely represent almost 24 percent of the labor force.[2]

Such changes in the workforce call for a consistent rather than a sporadic approach to diversity developments, as well as for appropriate resources and curriculum choices, which we will address.

"OLD" DIVERSITY CHALLENGES AND INCLUSION RESPONSES

Diversity models in the United States have historically been grounded in domestic issues arising from the government requirements and moral ground to redress past injustices and discrimination patterns, particularly against black people. Because of the resulting legal requirements and the tendency for companies to advertise their culture in ways that attract diverse prospective employees, most organizations project some commitment to diversity. Yet, we continue to learn that management is struggling with its diversity objectives and goals, in addition to its levels of diversity programming.[3] Even for companies such as IBM that have mature diversity initiatives and that proudly trace their diversity commitment and activities over three or more decades,[4] many globally expanding companies now have a need to consider a model of inclusion that can incorporate differences that exist within each of the national cultures they operate. DiversityInc, for example, continues to report on the demand by diversity leaders for information on global diversity best practices.[5]

Despite today's challenge, we acknowledge that many U.S. companies and foreign-owned companies operating in the U.S. have yet to develop organizational cultures that support even traditional, much less new, diversity commitments for various reasons. The U.S. Equal Employment Opportunity Commission's latest 2010 report showed a record number of discrimination suits, which reflects some inadequacies in compliance.[6] Most often, these reasons relate to prohibitive costs, an inability to measure results, and confusion as to what they need to do beyond matters of minimal legal and regulatory compliance. They might even relate to the assumption that biases cannot be fixed. And so, we offer the following value proposition, or our statement for achieving a higher level of effectiveness based on a new model of diversity, Transformational Diversity, using intercultural competence as its foundation.

TODAY'S DIVERSITY VALUE PROPOSITION

Corporate cultures and their corresponding values and assumptions such as quality and customer satisfaction, whether explicitly communicated or not, shape individual and group behaviors much in the same way that national cultural orientations influence the behavioral norms in societies; therefore, corporate cultures significantly determine workforce behaviors.[7] When corporate recruiters hire with particular skills and experiences in mind, they also look to hire based on an individual's ability to "fit in," that is, how easily the individual will adjust to the company's culture.[8] Adjusting is a form of "socializing" an individual to the corporate norms, values, and behaviors. "How we do things *here*," therefore, becomes a critical component of any company's organizational culture and performance expectations. Social scientists who have studied the process of cultural adjustment, in particular, claim that the adjustment process is easier when newcomers are culturally similar to the host culture, or to the corporate environment in this case. A related aspect to this adjustment or adaptation process is that it can have an effect on feelings of well being, which would include the absence or presence of stress.[9] Thus, while one may argue that new employees have a responsibility to make the effort to adjust to their new employer's culture, employers still need to minimize the risks that the adjustment process brings, such as extreme stress, which can result in poor performance. We recommend that employers try to minimize risks upfront in the recruiting process.

The "how" component of a company's behavior in today's global environment can become an organizational challenge for recruitment and even development due to changes in the cultural work orientations or backgrounds of the current and prospective employee base.[10] We note, for example, data that confirms what we are experiencing, that immigration into the U.S. has continued substantially over the past decade, thereby affecting our workforce composition (see Table 2.1).[11]

Projections for 2018 also reflect substantial changes in the racial and ethnic backgrounds of the U.S. population, as noted in Figure 2.2.[12]

According to one researcher, Michalle Mor Barak, the expanding workforce diversity continues to unveil one common factor — that of

Table 2.1: Population Change, by Nativity: 2000 and 2009

Universe: 2000 and 2009 resident population					
	2009 population	2000 population	Change, 2000-2009	Percent change, 2000-2009	Share of total change (%)
Native born	268,553,734	250,288,425	18,265,309	7.3	71.4
Foreign born	38,452,822	31,133,481	7,319,341	23.5	28.6
Total	307,006,556	281,421,906	25,584,650	9.1	100.0

Source: Pew Hispanic Center tabulations of 2000 Census (5% IPUMS) and 2009 American Community Survey (1% IPUMS).

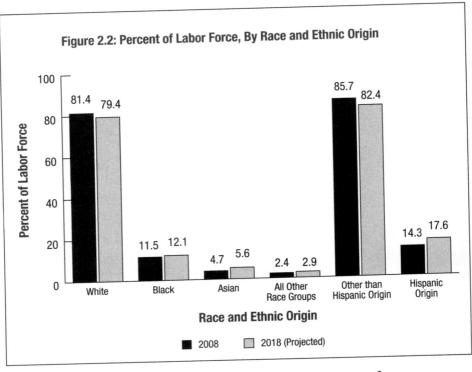

Figure 2.2: Percent of Labor Force, By Race and Ethnic Origin

social exclusion — even though diversity groupings may vary from one country to another.[13] In the case of the United States, we may view a rising tide of social exclusion by the confrontations between those in various political and social activities who equate the idea of the American dream with assimilation, versus those who may more visibly or actively support their immigrant or ethnic heritages as bicultural or multicultural. We need only to point to recent examples of anti-immigrant legislation as proposed in several U.S. states in 2010 (and made into law in Arizona, for instance). Therefore, corporate attention to this inclusion-exclusion issue on behalf of inclusion is pragmatic because it contributes to better performance. In this way, inclusion can become both the model and the de facto standard for organizations.

The challenges of these social changes can best be met through corporate preparedness and flexibility in addressing diversity issues that can lead an organization toward quantifiable and qualitative progress. In the past, company after company in the United States established diversity programming by first acknowledging the legal and moral pressures, and then by adding business cases focused on competitiveness and productivity.[14] They then set out to create organizational changes commensurate with culture change that followed a "template" of sorts, which more clearly allowed for some quantification of results and best-practice measurements.

At its core, the essence of diversity programming has ranged from being extremely broad to being categorically based on visible differences, to being a call for acceptance of all the ways individuals differ, without categorization. In this regard, the operating value of most diversity programming has become more U.S.-centric, especially if we think about its messages of egalitarianism, individualism, and achievement, which are considered core values of the United States by cultural scholars.[15] Not surprising, then, are the limits of this approach for companies operating in the global marketplace that increasingly hire multicultural workforces. Without a focus on differences from a research-supported cultural value basis and even on understanding different perspectives as to what constitutes "diversity" within environments, some of the current patterns of diversity activities will continue to provide a questionable return on investment (ROI). For only after rethinking the established diversity programming can we begin to work on bridging differences, which is more challenging than routinely acknowledging or managing them.

Above all, today's diversity value proposition calls for consistency provided by Transformational Diversity; it calls for a new perspective and, most importantly, for new action steps for organizational change. Foremost, it calls for an investment in training and education that introduces cultural awareness and dimensions that get to the core of different perspectives, and even, different behaviors. In this way, today's diversity value proposition requires education and training that mirror the workforce itself, from multicultural to multigenerational. While the "War for Talent," as first described by McKinsey Consultants in 1997[16] continues, today's battleground is on talent retention. The Transformational Diversity learning and development program that we propose can engage and help retain *all* employees. Moreover, it will provide them with skills in intercultural business competencies and communication that can help them better understand the origins of their conscious or unconscious biases, knowledge truly critical to the team-based environments in both domestic and international contexts.

The shift to Transformational Diversity also calls for organizational changes that can lead a company — through training — toward actively creating a culture of inclusion based on respect for cultural diversity. As with any change management initiative beyond leadership and other organizational development components, the power of transformation begins with some element of "introspection," or analysis, as companies identify and align their business activities with their diversity goals. All too often, companies fail in this aspect of the process since they assume that the very presence of extrinsic differences within its employee base is sufficient. However, each element of the work processes, including communication and information-sharing, decision-making, negotiation, management, and motivation, requires examination and redirection through the cultural diversity lens. In this way, biases can be exposed and reduced, while creativity and innovation, the hallmarks of diversity, can be released. Thus, developing and implementing "old" and "new" diversities simultaneously, not in a succession that places "new" diversity or intercultural training second, is, we believe, a part of a new diversity imperative within the framework of Transformational Diversity.

Regardless of a company's current stage of diversity programming, Transformational Diversity offers the ability to meet this imperative. Its suggested approach is twofold: first, it focuses on programming and learning solutions directed toward intercultural and therefore inclusive skill-building. In this way, going beyond the traditional domains of diversity such as age, race, and gender to include intercultural business competences is possible. Second, Transformational Diversity's approach incorporates organizational change programs that are behaviorally based and that address particular constituencies and employee groups through their business activities. These programs embrace both "old" (policy/state of mind) and "new" (action/intercultural business competencies and inclusive leadership training) diversity components — so that every organization can ensure a successful start from any point in its diversity developments.

Chapter 3. The *Why* of Transformational Diversity

This chapter will describe the background forces that pulled and pushed us to develop Transformational Diversity concepts and practices and will clarify the vision to explain and support it.

We will consider the business case for Transformational Diversity; the imperatives for change from "old" to Transformational Diversity in more detail; the new perspectives on "old" diversity; the upcoming new paradigm necessitating this switch; and finally how to set the stage for Transformational Diversity.

THE DRIVING FORCES

Let us now look at the background tendencies and forces that brought about Transformational Diversity. What are the historic necessities that condition further developing and extending of the initial concept of diversity today? What forces make it move to the new frontiers?

Globalization bears all the responsibility for changing the form of diversity we were accustomed to.[1] "Globalization," understood as one of the key ideas for business theory and practice, is commonly used for describing the connectedness of production, communication, and technologies across the world.

The results of globalization led to a reenergized and revamped diversity and inclusion concept, vision, setting of actions, and, of course, mentality to fit and carry out the new, higher goals.

Figure 3.1 offers the bigger picture of the Transformational Diversity background. First, as a deep-water, intangible background layer, with globalization, along come the former third-world countries — powerfully entering the international economy and competing for talent, creativity, and price.

The next layer at the backdrop is the driving forces of Transformational Diversity, all resulting from globalization and the technical progress of today's economy:

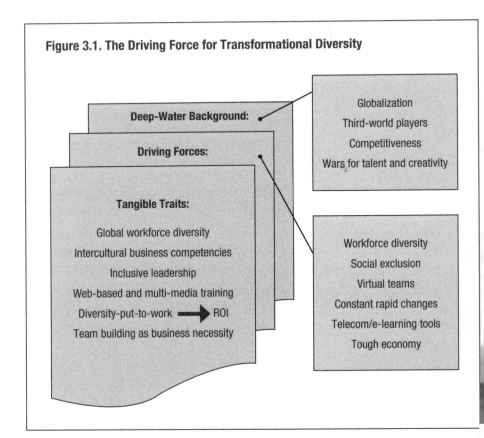

Figure 3.1. The Driving Force for Transformational Diversity

Deep-Water Background:

Driving Forces:

Tangible Traits:

Global workforce diversity
Intercultural business competencies
Inclusive leadership
Web-based and multi-media training
Diversity-put-to-work ➡ ROI
Team building as business necessity

Globalization
Third-world players
Competitiveness
Wars for talent and creativity

Workforce diversity
Social exclusion
Virtual teams
Constant rapid changes
Telecom/e-learning tools
Tough economy

- Increasingly diverse workforce, both locally and globally
- Social exclusion
- Virtual teams as a new reality that nobody can deny
- Constant rapid changes in all industries and organizations
- Outsourcing as fact and a need to leverage local and overseas employees
- Telecommunication, e-learning, and blended learning tools
- And, most importantly, formation of a new employee mentality that accepts all changes as positive but which may reflect a struggle as to how much of the old world will be left behind

One example of "social expulsion" or "social exclusion" follows.

Example. A member of a corporate diversity team of a large global organization works with a nonprofit organization as part of corporate outreach, helping it to self-organize and to develop social programs. She makes sure that the organization employees understand the importance of fair representation in their committee structure — thus replicating the familiar policy and practice of her firm. She is then taken aback when several people insist on excluding Arabs from representation on the committees because "they may be terrorists."

The Point. While prejudice often resides in misinformed populations, this example also suggests that the "numbers game" of traditional diversity only scratches the surface of what we need to address as better organizations building a better union. Transformational Diversity, with its focus on intercultural training, helps build a solid base for counteracting and neutralizing hostilities or misunderstandings alike and for building resistance to intolerance. While pockets of various types of social exclusion[2] of certain ethnic groups still exist in our country, this example signals for us the need for a driving force and an imperative for change.

Thus, the tough economic conditions of today may exacerbate all the driving forces mentioned above and call for action to deal with these issues.

REFLECTING ON THE DRIVING FORCES

The visible "tip of the iceberg" layer shows us the tangible traits of the newly emerging corporate diversity environment. Cultural complexity continues to be the hallmark of North American societies, which is why even domestic and pre-global organizations need to deal with intercultural communication issues that become especially compelling when selling to global markets. Companies whose management has the courage to show employees — and the world — that their inclusive working environment embraces teambuilding and develops all human capital will succeed globally. These companies educate their employees in inclusion, thus demonstrating advanced intercultural/interpersonal communication skills that will raise productivity, performance, and hence, return on investment. Transformational Diversity can be seen "live" in such companies.

Relevant data, published by the Society for Human Resource Management, are the "Top 10 Global Trends Most Likely to Have a Major Impact on the Workplace." We have listed six out of ten trends, as they refer to our topic:

1. Growing economic interdependence among world's countries (major strategic impact: 46 percent)

2. Increased expansion of U.S. companies into the global marketplace (major strategic impact: 46 percent)

3. Greater need for cross-cultural understanding/savvy in business settings (major strategic impact: 48 percent)

4. Economic growth of the BRIC (Brazil, Russia, India, China) emerging markets (major strategic impact: 53 percent)

5. Increased global competition (major strategic impact: 57 percent)

6. Overall decline in the workforce readiness of new entrants to the labor market in the United States as compared with other countries (major strategic impact: 58 percent)[3]

This data confirms our observations with respect to the "deep water" and "driving forces" background of Transformational Diversity as shown in Figure 3.1. Even with a quick look at the driving forces of Transformational Diversity, one thing is evident. In the United States we have — because of the economic momentum — an exceptional opportunity to help our organizations in shifting from traditional, "old" practices to Transformational Diversity. This change should be addressed holistically rather than focused piecemeal. Further analysis points out the actionable imperatives (identified as "Tangible Traits" in Figure 3.1) that will make our economy stronger and our workforce more competitive, which is the underlying purpose of this book.

THE PULL TO TRANSFORMATIONAL DIVERSITY

Explaining *why* we arrived at the Transformational Diversity idea and approach, we should first mention the *pull*. The vibe coming to us from corporate HR departments regarding their basic needs sounded loud and clear: the "old" diversity was becoming an antiquated, less meaningful approach, resulting in employee fatigue and marginal impact on business outcomes. At the same time, HR practitioners had difficulty in integrating issues attached to global diversity developments, for example, in how to align their traditional efforts with the global economic requirements of their businesses.[4] The toughest front for organizations seemed to be the integration of intercultural learning into the broader scheme of things.[5]

Thus, as diversity leaders were willing to try some new techniques to reawaken employee engagement, we as consultants were pulled in the Transformational Diversity direction and kept refining the content and format requirements as we progressed.

THE PUSH TO TRANSFORMATIONAL DIVERSITY

Among a number of different publications several years ago, a collection of articles in the *Wall Street Journal* most distinctly spelled out the need to advance diversity development.[6] The suggested goal, to embrace not only the U.S. workforce but also the globally minded and globally based workforce, closely matched what we were already doing. We started calling this approach "Diversity of Mind."

Our program offerings under the Diversity of Mind umbrella called for training and leadership development, tapping into cultural differences to capture new business and to deal with workplace diversity. The strategy was to unify a culturally and geographically diverse workforce. Going beyond traditional sensitivity training, the courses aimed to educate employees working virtually on the cultures of their overseas counterparts and U.S. employees on the diverse U.S.-American cultures. As we went along, we realized that the workforce and customer base of organizations was growing increasingly diverse and that consistent training courses could teach employees from different backgrounds to communicate better, to work more effectively as a team, and to serve a broad spectrum of customers more efficiently. Thus, progressively, the new vision of diversity developments came into being, and in 2008 we gave the approach a new name, Transformational Diversity. This reinvigorated approach had a mission — to revise "old" or traditional diversity programs through the addition of an intercultural perspective with intercultural business competencies training.

We do not focus on diversity of race or gender in a traditional sense but rather on diversity of intellectual orientation, ethnicity, communication styles, intercultural decision-making, and more.

EXAMPLE: INVISIBLE DIVERSITIES

A vice president of human resources from the manufacturing industry asked us to deliver one of our popular programs to his company's annual meeting of managers. When we agreed on a date for the presentation, he then hesitantly proceeded with, "Fiona, I don't know how to put it nicely ... you know how I respect you ... but the thing is that our upper management would prefer to invite a speaker with no foreign accent — please don't take it personally! This is their preference, not mine! So, could you send one of your consultants to us?" I was numb for a moment and then said "Yes, I can" again, with less enthusiasm, trying to make nothing of the remark. Later I thought it over, in a kind of self-debrief: What kind of diversity intolerance is that? What should we call it? Is it a "foreign accent phobia"?

The point. Many kinds of diversity exist that must be addressed to mitigate intolerance in the workplace. We all need to work actively against all forms of dominance, subordination, and humiliation that undermine the ability of even the most talented individuals to bring 100 percent of their creative ideas to the workplace.

Organizations of all kinds face a growing challenge of dealing with invisible and intangible intolerance. First and foremost, we need practical inclusion-boosting programs for all employees, and these should integrate different intercultural competencies. According to a 2008 survey by Novations, a Boston-based consulting group, over 40 percent of organizations expanded the scope of their inclusion programs in connection with globalization — up from 15 percent in 2005.[7] This increase may be an appropriate response to the changing demographics of the workforce, but is it appropriate enough? Or is it good enough?

EXAMPLE: VOICING YOUR OPINION

A well-established global company from the chemical industry regularly spent tremendous amounts of money organizing its regional and local diversity conferences. These events were routinely attended by senior executives. As invited speakers, we attended one of the regional conferences and could not help but notice that intercultural issues were given scant attention as compared to the interest they inspired, with many participants asking for more workshops in the future. This lack of awareness on the part of conference organizers reflected the general corporate insufficiency, intentional or not, to provide possible solutions for many misunderstandings and disputes among employees of this diverse corporation. To this effect, a senior vice president closed the conference telling 350 attendees "to never hesitate to come forward and report if you notice inadequate management behavior or any need or possibility for improvement." The men sitting next to us discussed it in low voices: "Does he take me for a fool or what? I've worked here for 12 years and can well imagine the consequences, especially with my current boss." So the call for coming forward and participating may not be enough.

The point. The above-mentioned company is well on track as far as traditional diversity programming goes. However, it may need to do even more toward creating a culture of inclusion because funding affinity groups and conferences alone does not fit the bill.

FOSTERING HIGH-PERFORMANCE CORPORATE CULTURE

Another area for creating new programs includes bridging cultural differences for fostering a high-performance corporate culture in a novel way. The whole host of these programs, covered further in the book, address intercultural influencing, decision-making, negotiating, internal and external communication, generational mentality, intellectual orientations, and work styles, among still other aspects of difference.

As we can see, intercultural competencies of all kinds have a broad scope of application and relevance. These are two of the characteristics of Transformational Diversity.

THE BUSINESS CASE FOR TRANSFORMATIONAL DIVERSITY

HR professionals strive every day to implement "best" practices at their respective organizations. And this is why Transformational Diversity matters. It *is* the best practice on the diversity horizon today, and the reason becomes clear when we consider the business case for Transformational Diversity.

The arguments for a diversity and inclusion business case[8] typically fall into four or five categories,[9] and the most frequently cited argument[10] — increasing internal efficiency — is in fact a business outcome argument: improvements to business outcome go further when the workforce is diverse. Clearly, they also go the furthest when the workforce is trained — not just told — to be efficient team members. This is where Transformational Diversity comes in. By definition, it is a new diversity brand, one that revises traditional diversity programming by embracing an intercultural perspective using intercultural competencies training while focusing on a workplace culture that is inclusive, which is the most significant contributor to teamwork and increased efficiency. Inclusivity in the workplace is the bottom-line emphasis that comes to the forefront.

To start, Table 3.1 offers the definitions, attributes, and organizational applications of diversity and inclusion.

Table 3.1

Attributes of Diversity and Inclusion Practices	
• Diversity – a state of mind: existence of and response to many diverse cultural groups	• Inclusion – action: practices and behaviors that value and promote differences
Organizational Applications	
• Complies with national laws • Actively recruits and develops people who are different • Promotes behaviors based on established standards • Has no cultural bias in HR management systems and practices • Recognizes "opening doors and minds" as important awareness • Promotes affinity groups.	• Fosters and values cultural differences • Considers and respects all cultures and their values • Helps employees develop commonalities with people different from themselves • Reveals and diminished unconscious biases • Increasingly, means "working in a cooperative, inclusive, respectful way" in spite of and because of differences • Develops inter-group harmony to enhance productivity & ROI.

Differentiating between diversity (the state of mind) and inclusion (the action, practices, and behaviors) is essential for planning organizational applications for both of them. In the left column of the table we see the organizational applications for traditional diversity practice, or "diversity programming templates," which typically include legal and regulatory compliance, support of affinity groups of all kinds, recruitment of minorities, a bias-free HR management system, promotion of behaviors based on certain standards, and such.

In the right column are the underutilized applications for inclusion. Fostering cultural differences and respecting all cultures and their values are the most common. The next three applications are the most practical and useful of all.

The business case for Transformational Diversity is simple: it centers its attention on inclusion because inclusive cultures foster higher employee engagement. Engaged, motivated employees produce better results and report increased job satisfaction, which has a direct impact on profitability.

While many people understand the meaning of diversity, only few realize the impact that inclusion has on the bottom line of business. To plumb the issue further, according to Gallup Workplace Studies, companies that are effective in creating an inclusive environment saw remarkable business advantages when compared with the companies that are not effective. In particular, Gallup reported the following results:

- Customer satisfaction increase by 39 percent

- Productivity increase by 22 percent

- Profitability increase by 27 percent

- Turnover decrease by 22 percent[11]

The data virtually speaks for itself. Even if we put aside the tangible financial results, an inclusive environment can also be a great source of employee engagement. That type of inclusive atmosphere may certainly bring forth more creative ideas, support risk-taking, and lead to the production of world-class goods and services.[12] These outcomes will inevitably contribute to the success of a company's domestic and global market share as well as to its own increased corporate value.

But now the question arises: *How* do we more effectively activate the potential of inclusion as action? How do we transcend the already existing applications of "old" diversity that would *not* let the new approach of Transformational Diversity take hold? To adopt a new mode of operating while integrating inclusion with the established traditional diversity practices is no easy matter. This transition to the new kind of practices is central to this book.

Let us think for a moment of the alternative: diversity/inclusion *depreciation or decline*. What happens? The best and the brightest employees leave; morale declines; creativity gets stifled; team spirit vanishes or exists in name only; and a discriminatory work environment emerges, along with increasing exposure to lawsuits and plummeting business value. Additionally, since "Diversity is a cultural issue within companies"[13] the internal resistance to all diversity efforts can grow exponentially, along with hiring, promoting, and integrating a critical mass of employees from diverse backgrounds — which is now universally considered to be a backbone of organizational innovation and overall success.

Our business case for Transformational Diversity rests on our own experiences and observations, as well as on the most recent research in the field. The business case for diversity typically has several main overlapping components, namely the following:

- Tapping into a broader range of backgrounds and skill sets to guarantee a larger talent pool for the future (53 percent)

- Instilling a fairness and moral imperative — ensuring an equal chance for members of disadvantaged groups (47 percent)

- Mirroring the customer base at the workplace to better understand customers and grow sales (43 percent)

- Being mindful of the diversity of both customers and suppliers (42 percent)

- Ensuring legal compliance (38 percent)[14]

Currently a documented, quantitative link between greater diversity/inclusion and an improved bottom line that is universally recognized does not exist.[15] The diversity of the employee base certainly gives us the opportunity to achieve a much-sought-after diversity of mind: the team that generates ten different business solutions to the same issue has more choices and improves its ability to arrive at an innovative decision. This subject, known as the "Medici Effect," is the point at which creativity and innovation results from the intersection of different perspectives of people from different disciplines and cultures.[16] Nonetheless, the benefits of diversity remain hard to quantify in HR terms: for instance, how do you measure trust and confidence in the operation, improved mutual understanding, a sense of partnership among employees, or synergy between the team members? Many phenomena in social sciences are hard to measure or even accurately define due to their fluid nature as well as to the constantly evolving perspectives of the users.

Some HR professionals, as well as other business leaders, believe the connection between ROI and the bottom line and diversity results is disputable because it is often difficult to quantify, yet they do agree on the perceived qualitative correlation to business performance. Not surprisingly, the role of best practices in diversity and inclusion as benchmarks is therefore important and prominent, since these benchmarks also serve as a basis of measurement in lieu of quantifiable data.[17]

As mentioned in Chapter 1, the research commissioned by SHRM from the Economist Intelligence Unit, indicates that 500 prominent global executives surveyed still think that this correlation of ROI and inclusion is of a qualitative, not quantitative nature. Our thought, though, is that a qualitative contribution to the bottom line is a contribution all the same, even if intuitive and not empirical in most cases. With Transformational Diversity's special-purpose training, the improved workforce synergy goes a long way toward positively transforming workplace behaviors while adding to the bottom line.

NEW PERSPECTIVES ON "OLD" DIVERSITY AND IMPERATIVES FOR CHANGE

This section is a logical continuation of the business case for Transformational Diversity; here we provide more clarity on why established diversity programming either no longer fits the bill or is working and how the "old diversity" can change and incorporate what is "new," as we characterize it. We conclude with our views on today's imperatives for change. As argued before, Transformational Diversity alters current diversity programs with its cross-cultural perspective offering intercultural training to broad employee populations. Its goal is to form leadership and workplace culture that is inclusive. It certainly represents a shift in traditional diversity developments, a necessary shift that may be long overdue.

ESTABLISHED DIVERSITY PROGRAMMING AND TEMPLATES NO LONGER FIT THE BILL

Example. A prominent European bank has its U.S. headquarters in New York and offices all over North and South America. To cover its diversity compliance issues, the bank set up its diversity department and hired two lawyers to do the job. Evidently, the lawyers addressed the task as well as they could: they hired a traditional diversity consultant firm to cover the "old" diversity programming. Despite the fact that the organizational development consultant pointed out the need for inclusive mindset development through intercultural competencies training and for a special interest group for numerous expatriates from Europe, these recommendations were never followed. Meanwhile, the expats started self-organizing themselves, in get-togethers after hours, excursions, and parties, thus remaining an isolated group. At the same time, the domestic employees maintained their stereotyped views of the expatriates as elitist snobs who would never blend in.

The point. The need of the employees from nondominant ethnicities to reach some comfort level sharing experiences and assimilating to a degree — for business ends — exists. This need is most significant and urgent for the expatriates. The necessary shift to inclusion practices is long overdue in this global bank. Although management made a shortcut bowing to "old" diversity, the proposed changes were not put into practice, an outcome increasingly derided by employees who often shrug their shoulders when summoned to diversity training, typically on compliance issues. Diversity shortcuts are not enough any longer; people are longing for inclusion, and we need to strive toward creating an inclusive culture, especially if we want the workforce to be truly effective.

We have already drawn attention to the fact that diversity management in the United States has remained challenged, and some say "tired." Some diversity professionals recognize that diversity initiatives backfire, often fostering tensions and hindering corporate performance, and in general "diversity efforts are not fulfilling their promise."[18] Although some diversity professionals may think they have done enough and need to do nothing different, their performance has achieved the desired outcomes, as recent research pointed out. The truth is that the potential of even the best-in-diversity North American companies, however established their diversity programming may be, is not fulfilled: it is measured at only 61.5 to 70 percent of the total potential.[19] But there is more to it than untapped potential because the employees may start doubting the value of diversity programming in general — which may undermine even the essential fairness concept that diversity was originally built upon; this should not happen and we need to make more efforts addressing it.

Established diversity programming and its existing templates or benchmarks no longer fit the bill, as people are tired of them for many reasons. Such perceptions of traditional diversity practices developed over time, and nowadays people are often critical of them.

SIMULTANEOUS DEVELOPMENT OF "OLD" AND "NEW" DIVERSITY

Introducing Transformational Diversity and dropping "old" practices do not involve ideological confrontational strategies — because the "new" and "old" diversity practices are not contradictory. We believe that the companies with established diversity programming need to leapfrog to meet the new multicultural, diverse workforce needs and to achieve Transformational Diversity — and then continue developing both aspects simultaneously. However, the company that starts diversity work from scratch should not necessarily start with the old, comfortable diversity first and then proceed to the new Transformational Diversity developments. That method may take years and cost a lot of money along the way.

Example. A pharmaceutical company sustained four diversity teams within six years. The first team was considered inexperienced by the new management and was let go. The second team consisted of professionals who brought a wealth of experience to the company. Their secure strategy was to properly develop diversity as they had done it for years: first establish policies and then affinity groups, and then secure the upper management buy-in worldwide. They told us, "Your training on inclusion is very good; we'll use it later, but we must first follow these other steps." Guess what? "Later" never came. That diversity team moved fast and spent a lot of effort and money unrolling the traditional diversity action steps worldwide. However, upon failing to achieve a favorable return on investment, the team was disbanded after about three years. The third team was filled by company insider(s) who criticized the previous team as big spenders; the director of diversity was coached by the CEO himself. However, the team's lack of constructive ideas and action led to moving all training to the learning department and diversity-oriented leadership matters to the leadership division. Initially, this no-action tactic helped the team stay in place for two years — then it too was gone. The times changed, and in a tough economy upper management had little patience. Then the new, fourth team reinvented the company's diversity strategy and programs all over again. For the time being, we are approaching the company's situation philosophically now and waiting to see what diversity path they will next take: the beaten path of "old" diversity, or no action, or the Transformational Diversity path.

The point. Transformational Diversity should be regarded as a new brand, a renaissance of traditional diversity, one that helps us move quickly with the times in a novel way and to demonstrate practical results with positive impact on the bottom line, while not totally sacrificing the established practices. It appears that this new path, a path of action, is the secure path.

IMPERATIVES FOR CHANGE

Transformational Diversity is all about positive change, which is why we call it "transformational." It delivers change in diversity practices by definition: it changes current diversity programs through a critical-mass infusion of an intercultural standpoint coupled with intercultural education. As a new, in-step-with-the-times modification of diversity, it takes the old practices beyond race and gender, shifting the focus from traditional race-gender issues to minorities-integration-synergy-performance issues as well as to inclusive leadership issues. Transformational Diversity initiatives are also about talent and organizational development. As we are well aware, many organizations in the United States employ a diverse workforce — which is an upswing tendency, and the diversity efforts need to be coordinated with organizational developments, hence the key word: *transformation.* This transformation, or positive change, implies more radical change in focus and practices. Of course, nobody *really* likes change (it is only human not to.) With respect to this dislike of change, we love how Winston Churchill put it, famously, "While everybody likes to be in heaven, nobody wants to die."

So whether we want change or not, we must urgently act now. We have identified five imperatives for change, some of which incorporate newer realities, as follows.

Imperative 1: Need to Align Domestic Efforts to Increasingly Multicultural Workforce and Develop Global Diversity Initiatives

Not only global but also domestic efforts on diversity should do more to target the increasingly multicultural workforce. According to U.S. government statistics, in 2030 the United States will have a population of approximately 400 million people. This means that every 20 seconds a new immigrant arrives in the United States. Practically speaking, these numbers mean that intercultural business competencies training should be put in place and customized according to respective organizational cultures. This need, however, is often overlooked by diversity practitioners who choose to ignore the fact of growing multiculturalism because taking action would mean going beyond their comfortable traditional-diversity zone.

Example. In our mission to promote the implementation of Transformational Diversity, we reached out to a diversity vice president at a global pharmaceutical company by introducing intercultural business competencies programs as the means to achieve better inclusion. Admitting that this was a good idea, she noted that the company does not need any new programs and explained why it is happy with its current performance, because, after all, the company's diversity programming consistently ranks in the top 10 in the United States. For many years the company has used an online tool for cultural diversity that it believed covered the global cross-cultural space. We responded that the tool, a well-known self-assessment questionnaire, was helpful but insufficient as a standalone, without a supporting subsequent cross-cultural debrief or training. However, we never heard back from the company.

The point. Overall, the diversity field is steeped in tradition, and diversity leaders may not be easily propelled into action, regardless of what noble cause or potential business outcome could result from it. How can we overcome this resistance to all things new? The key is for top leadership to realize the necessity of this transformation to promote intercultural training, which will develop an inclusive mindset and enhance business outcomes.

Imperative 2: Need to Compete in the War for Talent Creating Corporate-Wide Culture of Inclusion

The war for talent continues to escalate globally; it is a reality of today's business landscape. Whether we recruit locally — or in Dubai, Mumbai, or Shanghai — the attractiveness of a corporate-wide culture of inclusion (resulting from Transformational Diversity efforts) will help us win and retain the best talent. As organizations continue to draw an assorted pool of employees from cultures all over the world, inclusive leadership culture is the best way to handle the workforce's ever-changing demographics. The relentless pursuit of the best talent increasingly involves multicultural talent. Organization leaders need not only meet and greet their new talent with open arms but also install them in a culture-sensitive, inclusive leadership environment where they will be encouraged to give their loyalty and productivity 100 percent — instead of isolating them because they feel like "foreign bodies" in the mainstream organizational culture. Certainly, organizations cannot afford to be left unprepared to deal with issues that stand in the way of the company becoming productive, stable, and more effective.[20] Evidently, creating a corporate-wide culture of inclusion is the company's only guarantee in winning the war for talent and also in keeping this talent creative and productive. Unfortunately, more often than not, shaping an inclusive corporate culture remains largely a vague promise, and the new hires as well as expatriates feel uncomfortable and confused for too long.

Example. Anne, an HR generalist, was transferred from Germany to the U.S. subsidiary of a global pharmaceutical company. She participated in a "Communicating with People Who Speak English as a Second Language" program. During the debrief, she shared that if she had known "the rules of the game" in communicating with U.S.-American colleagues, she would have been spared much of the embarrassment and confusion she felt during her first year in the United States; in particular, she had difficulty getting used to people using so many sports terms in everyday conversations. She provided an example of the time her manager said, "Anne, we'll touch base later." She said she immediately panicked, thinking "Touch what? Why me? What did I do?" It took her a while to get used to this communication style and to feel more comfortable and included, not threatened.

The point. When we bring new talent from abroad to the company, if we truly care about their workplace satisfaction, we should not only educate them in general about living and working in the United States — which should be a must — but also educate the locals about other cultures and the ways they can make it easier for the international employees to fit in and to perform at their maximum level of productivity. This is all about inclusion and inclusive leadership culture. We all should be concerned about growing, not shrinking, our talent base, and our focus on diversity/inclusion along the entire workforce pipeline ensures a supply of the best-qualified, diverse candidates.

Imperative 3: Need to Develop Inclusion-Oriented Systematic Education

This imperative is, in fact, a corollary of the second imperative because education, training, and employee development are the means for developing inclusive organizational cultures. People do not naturally demonstrate inclusive behaviors — so employees need to work through *how* and *why* other people behave differently. This in-depth understanding of others leads to respect of others, and respect is the only way that will lead to synergy and true teamwork in the workplace. Let us provide an example of the benefits of intercultural education for both employees and managers.

Example. This case was shared by a young manager in her first corporate job. She was surrounded by other colleagues, each in his or her own cubicle. Her neighbor, Bob, a software team leader, was a well-liked manager. Customarily, before the December holiday, the U.S.-American programmers who reported to him often approached him to discuss bonuses or raises. They were not shy about asking for what they wanted, pointing out how hard they had worked and what projects they had completed — and Bob often agreed. Once, a young talent, a star Chinese programmer, came over to Bob and said: "Well,

Bob, you know that I accomplished two important projects, worked really hard, and completed project X on time and that the results surprised even the president ... I never said no when you needed me to work on Saturdays ... I hope you remember that." And with this he left. Bob wondered, "What is he after? Does he want to be acknowledged in front of the team? That's easy; I'll do that." And he did just that. Bob was really surprised when that star programmer left for another company in March.

The point. The Chinese-American programmer did not say directly that he too wanted a well-deserved bonus because in his culture many employees of Chinese descent do not put such requests in words to a manager, who is their senior. The right way to attract and retain talent while building a truly inclusive culture is to educate all managers and employees about cultural differences and various communication styles.

By "systematic" education we mean two things. First, education does not need to stay within the traditional confines of the training department, but rather other divisions of the organization need to become involved by helping fund and sponsor the trainings so that all of them get credit for accomplishing a good initiative. Second, "systematic" also means that education should not be sporadic in any way but should be taken seriously by organizational management. The systematic approach may also be called "seamless," and seamlessness is yet another crucial element for Transformational Diversity.

It is noteworthy that 500 global executives surveyed placed a great premium on education efforts to promote and monitor diversity and inclusion. Thus, 40 percent of them say they are using "employee development and training to enhance respect for cultural and other differences among colleagues," and 26 percent are even "offering language courses to increase awareness of other cultures and promote communication."[21] As we can see, Transformational Diversity is in accord with these important tendencies.

Imperative 4: Need to Minimize the Layoff Aftermath

Organizations have an urgent need to minimize the drastic effects of a landslide of layoffs in 2008 and 2009 and of the sluggish recovery thereafter. Their aftermath resulted in the plummeting morale and productivity of the "layoff survivors": when one's confidence in job security is sagging, often one's productivity also sags. In many instances, transforming morale and productivity is key to survival, so consequently, the efforts to mollify the aftereffects of a company-wide layoff should be a cornerstone strategy. Not surprisingly, the consequences for human capital in terms of plunging morale after mergers and acquisitions are similar to those after layoffs — these situations also call for the attention of diversity leaders, human resources, and management.

The November 2008 issue of *HR Magazine* discussed the feelings of insecurity and guilt experienced by layoff survivors after an exodus of employees.[22] The effects of layoffs on surviving employees continue to be a serious issue. HR professionals along with senior management often tend to pay more attention to those employees who received pink slips than to those who stayed. However, when the layoffs hit the workplace, the victims are not only those who got fired: the layoff survivors feel victimized too, and "layoff survivor sickness" is alive and well, crippling the company's productivity.

Research has shown that layoff survivor sickness brings about emotions such as anxiety, insecurity, frustration, anger, depression, guilt, betrayal, and distrust.[23] What is the end result? Some people are so struck by their organization's "unfairness" that they would leave their company at the first opportunity, so subsequent downsizing turnover (of the most valued employees) is inevitable. In a tough economy this effect may be lingering, but inevitable anyway. This situation signals an immediate threat to a company's well being, especially coming right after layoffs. Why? In part, survivors worrying about their future are very risk-averse, en masse. Yet, these companies rely on employees' risk-taking and on their superior decision-making skills to generate new revenue to stay afloat. Additionally, the factor of flagging employee loyalty can — if left unattended — result in harmful information leaks to competitors, the public, or the media; unfortunately, there are many recent cases of such leaks.

The question often asked is the following: How can we buffer the negative effect of downsizing on our best remaining human capital? Certain HR practices can help mitigate employee stress by offering programs that give people a feeling that their organization is just and fair overall and, most importantly, that it cares about them. Some HR consultants have recommended extending defined benefit plans, onsite child care, sabbaticals, options to work from home, and flextime to employees — which may sometimes be costly or impossible for the particular company's work environment.[24]

One solution that counteracts layoff survivor sickness and that fits absolutely all types of companies is training; providing specific training to promote employees' growth on the job today shows them that their companies do care about them. In connection with this solution, diversity departments need to considerably extend their training offerings and work hand in hand with training and development departments, even sharing the funding when necessary.

Social science and HR professionals are unanimous in their recommendation for companies that want to survive after layoffs and retain talent; the best thing to do is something very visible. What can be more visible and induce synergetic team behaviors more than intercultural business competencies training for all employees? The answer is nothing! Training is the most effective tool to ease the stress of layoff survivor syndrome because, by definition, team-building and inclusion-oriented trainings are respectful of all differences and often become the key drivers of workplace behavior. Best of all, training is a subtle, indirect solution; on some basic level it ensures the perception of fairness in restructuring decisions while facilitating "venting" or, in other words, externalizing the survivor feelings and helping people to move forward into performance as usual. The Transformational Diversity training effectively and powerfully helps refocus employees, offers them new tools for making an impact on the job, and gives them a reason to stay. It also shows them that the organization and its management *care* about them in all seriousness, providing training for teamwork, better communication skills, improved leadership skills, mutual understanding, and support. This is why the Transformational Diversity initiative always results in enhanced productivity backed by employee loyalty during tough times, when all businesses, big and small, need both productivity and loyalty the most.

We believe that taking care of this situation and people should be entrusted to and become the responsibility of diversity departments. Why? Because the U.S. workforce is one of the most diverse in the world, and diversity departments traditionally took care of those underappreciated and underserved, in other words — the "underdogs." Diversity managers are the ones who need to take charge of sagging employee morale using the tools of Transformational Diversity to enrich or galvanize traditional practices that failed to address the current situation.

Imperative 5: Need to Be Socially Responsible

The recent global economic crises, regardless of any analysis as to their origins, have exposed various excesses and failures by corporate leaders with regard to social responsibility. By social responsibility, we mean how an organization chooses to do its business and to make its money in consideration of its impact on a broader environment, meaning its larger society and economy. It is not just the question of impact and consideration of particular stakeholders such as shareholders, employees, and clients. We believe that diversity leadership is a ripe arena for redeeming the washed-out image of business leaders, and the time for action is now. Indeed, many European organizations have already seized this opportunity. We need only look to Belgium, the Netherlands, and Germany, where despite their internal disruptions in recent years arising from accelerated immigration, corporate leadership is actively working on behalf of equality and inclusion. Regardless of certain limitations to their successes, their efforts have placed their organizations in the forefront by taking responsibility to change for the better. The United States and Europe differ on many matters of diversity and inclusion.[25] However, we believe there is much to value and emulate in the efforts of the European-style alignment of corporate responsibility with diversity issues.

SETTING THE STAGE

While setting the stage for the rollout of Transformational Diversity, we need to be clear: Transformational Diversity is needed now more than ever because in tough times and competitive markets we need to capitalize on a broader human capital pool while developing, nurturing, optimizing, and retaining the best talent. The two major outcomes of Transformational Diversity are inclusive leadership and intercultural business competencies — both of which have proved to be critical for improving productivity and performance of organizations. We will clarify both outcomes below.

Step One. Understanding the Pragmatic Outcomes

At this stage, prior to the rollout of Transformational Diversity we need to prioritize its goals. They can be summarized as follows:

- Contribution to enhanced productivity and performance

- Visible inclusion-boosting necessary to win the war for talent

- Transformation of corporate culture to fit the latest societal and economic paradigm shift toward multiculturalism

- Mitigating intolerance to enhance local and global teamwork and productivity

- Making an observable connection between domestic/pre-global and globalized diversity efforts

Testing the waters with a number of Transformational Diversity pilot sessions can become the basis of taking the next step.

Step Two. Leadership Buy-In on Major Outcomes and on Inclusive Leadership in Particular

Upper management buy-in and total continual support are absolutely necessary. Since two major outcomes of Transformational Diversity are inclusive leadership culture and intercultural business competencies on a broad scale, gaining the approval of top management is essential for success: Without leadership approval nothing can be accomplished. Moreover, leadership needs to actively support the development of both an inclusive leadership organizational culture and intercultural business competencies.

Transformational Diversity seamlessly incorporates intercultural learning and then centers on intercultural business competencies. These naturally call for inclusive leadership development, which plays into teambuilding and enhanced performance. The concept of inclusive leadership is a critical aspect effecting today's culture in transformative ways. Our goal is not to analyze different definitions of inclusive leadership here; however, we will draw on some groundbreaking research on the subject by J. Ryan and E. P. Hollander.[26]

Inclusive leadership supporting diversity is a new and powerful development. Inherent in this intentionally inclusive practice is a value of and respect for all cultures encompassing all types of differences. Inclusive leadership is a process that incorporates both leaders who influence and their influenced followers; it places human relationships on center stage and sees the purpose of the organization beyond purely financial goals. Inclusive leadership mindset is accepting that "democracy is not a spectator sport," as Arianna Huffington remarked,[27] and that no fundamental change can be accomplished without involving broader, wider circles of human capital. We add that it is necessary to persuade organizations and all stakeholders to train/coach human capital *how* to be more inclusive leaders to make the system functional, again. More specifically, inclusive leadership involves respectful service to people above self-interest, reasonable restraints in the use of power, and concern for both the sustainable development of employees and the cohesiveness of the whole organization. It also applies, more broadly, to individuals and organizations, rather than just to managers and executives. Inclusive leaders set themselves as models based on their own self-awareness; they are also activists on behalf of the powerful potential of diverse perspectives and contributions. They lead or manage with a mindfulness that allows differences in and keeps exclusion out. Since inclusion and leadership attitudes, skills, and behaviors are learned — not inborn — developing inclusive leaders is fundamental to Transformational Diversity initiatives training.

We need to remember the connection between inclusive leadership development and intercultural communication skills. The role of communication as a leadership and corporate culture change issue cannot be overemphasized. First, communication is often intended to influence and manipulate people. Inclusive leadership, however, involves influencing, partly by example, partly through communication — and here leaders are heavily dependent on language; however, when the speaker and the listener are from different cultures, the odds against an accurate interpretation of the message are great. Diverse communication styles, traditions, and cultural taboos all interfere with comprehension and make accurate understanding arbitrary.

Second, the concept of leadership varies across cultures.[28] Evidence shows that expectations of what leaders should be like and what they should do differ across continents and cultures, and global companies must duly address this dissimilarity.

Third, to be an inclusive, global leader one has to learn and understand how to motivate an increasingly diverse workforce, which is impossible without culturally sensitive communication. Each language has certain in-built characteristics, often unperceived by the people who speak them. Thus, leaders need to be trained to communicate with people (both from their own culture and from other cultures) in a culturally sensitive manner for them to be perceived as inclusive and respectful of all differences and for their human capital to feel inspired and motivated. In fact, we believe that intercultural communication courses for inclusion should be a part of all leadership development and Transformational Diversity courses.

Fourth, and most importantly, inclusive leadership has a defined business value achieved specifically through communication. Carol Bartz, CEO of Yahoo!, maintains that inclusive leadership is "one of the best paths to new insights."[29] Moreover, leaders have an obligation to identify thought leaders — people with the ability to digest and interpret information for others — and to groom them to help foster a culture of openness and creativity, the greatest energy an organization can have. These four factors explain much of why Transformational Diversity leadership development courses focus on inclusion-oriented communication, opening the door to embrace a corporate culture of inclusion.

Our analysis and experiences in Transformational Diversity point to the relationship between inclusive leadership, communication, and diversity. This relationship is why Transformational Diversity makes a point of incorporating inclusive leadership and continuous learning as the ways that motivate talent to stay and perform to their full potential. HR professionals need to be inclusive leaders as well. An accumulation of these intercultural communication skills can translate into the tangible results we seek.

Step Three. A Clear Understanding of What Intercultural Business Competencies Bring to Organizations at Large

As we have already mentioned, Transformational Diversity is about intercultural competence as an urgent business imperative in our push for productivity. We scoured some sources to see how others define intercultural competence, for example at Kwintessential, a global translation and cultural communications firm, we read that it is more than just the ability to work well across cultures.[30] Thus intercultural competence may be described as the following:

• Overall capability to manage key challenging features of intercultural communication, namely cultural differences and unfamiliarity, inter-group dynamics, and the tensions and conflicts that can accompany this process[31]

- Abilities to perform effectively and appropriately with members of another language-culture background on their terms[32]

- Ability to interact with people different from you in a genuinely constructive manner which is free of negative attitudes (e.g., prejudice, defensiveness, apathy, aggression etc.); the ability to create a synthesis, something which is neither "mine" nor "yours," but which is genuinely new and would not have been possible had we not combined our different backgrounds and approaches[33]

We would like to add to the above definitions the ability to change or adapt one's behaviors as appropriate. These (and many other) definitions of intercultural competence refer to communication abilities. Keeping these definitions in mind, let us reiterate the main statement of this book: we believe that the focus of diversity efforts should shift to inclusion and to intercultural business competencies training so that diversity becomes more practical and relevant in relation to today's workforce and economic climate. This is the change we need to help our economy and our country succeed. This change, or transformation, is not just a dream, but it becomes doable when we make use of the right tools. We will present a succinct description of some of these tools in the last chapter of this book.

Chapter 4. The *What* of Transformational Diversity

This chapter will identify strategies and some concrete, actionable steps for HR leaders who want to transform their diversity programs and initiatives. We have previously stated our reasoning as to why change in diversity activities needs to take place. Here we turn to offering specifics, which we consider to be the *What* of Transformational Diversity.

We start with some general strategies that may not be entirely familiar to all diversity practitioners. We consider these to be the basic ingredients in our recipe for successful change. To bring about change we suggest four areas for strategic focus and planning:

- *Stressing values.* This area recognizes values as the drivers of differential behaviors in the workplace.

- *Focusing on differences of relevance or consequence.* Perhaps diversity programs would have more success if organizations concentrated on selected dimensions of difference or on only those of consequence to their ability to do business.

- *Aligning domestic diversity with a global perspective.* All domestic diversity programs should align with a global perspective, whether or not the organization has yet to launch a global diversity initiative.

- *Developing intercultural sensitivity organization-wide.* The teaching of intercultural sensitivity skills should extend throughout the organization after diversity leaders have acquired an understanding of the overall developmental nature of culture change when applied to organizations.

Next, we offer some specific areas of corporate intervention as a basis for action.

TRANSFORMATIONAL DIVERSITY: GENERAL STRATEGIES

Training and Development

To effect change in the direction of the transformation of diversity programs, we believe that an organization must first commit to a strategy or plan that focuses on training and development as the means to that end. Training should be an essential component of organizational effectiveness and performance efforts. It is the basis that allows organizations to continue operating, and in many instances, it is the key to its survival. HR thought leaders remind us that education through training and development needs to be a fundamental strategy for all business and strategic-planning activities.[1]

Within the context of diversity strategy, we believe that as an initial strategy, a commitment to training and development in diversity must be real, targeted in content, and reach everyone in the organization.

In reality, current diversity practices seem to place training last rather than first in priority. Too often organizations implement diversity training that is remedial — perhaps as a result of a discrimination suit or the fear of one? The mere presence of a diverse workforce, whether acquired naturally or through targeted recruiting efforts, does not guarantee success. We must be educated in behaving inclusively and respectfully toward others who are different from us; these behaviors are learned attributes. If we are not taught, we can be left defending our positions and opinions to the point of conflict. We may look easily to the broader society and to its institutions such as educational systems, family life, and religious organizations and to even history for the sources of intolerance and bias. Yet, when diverse populations converge in the workplace, corporations and their HR leaders need to determine and require acceptable behavior of employees. Being "politically correct" is still a serious matter, despite its sometimes being the source of humor. Organizations need to socialize or educate employees on the "right" social and workplace inclusive behaviors. Our experiences show that success in this effort can be accomplished through training and development strategies committed to diversity and inclusion.

Defining Diversity and Inclusion through Values

Our second general strategy calls for using a values-based approach in defining diversity. Any strategy for diversity must have a mindfulness that calls for understanding the *breadth* of differences, which is what is meant by inclusion. However, when dealing with the topic of diversity, all organizations must first offer a definition of what they mean by diversity and inclusion so that their attributes are clear and can lead to positive outcomes.

We find that most definitions can be, in our opinion, either narrow or broad. Narrow definitions, on the one hand, tend to list specific categorizations or dimensions. In the U.S. environment, and increasingly in the European one, these are usually identified as gender, race and ethnicity, national origin, disability, age, and sexual orientation. Broad definitions, on the other hand, are less specific and contain very general words about respect for "visible and invisible differences" or "all the ways we differ." Readers are encouraged to visit any number of corporate websites to consider examples of these two definitional approaches.

Each approach has consequences that are not always positive. The first approach of narrow definitions is subject to micromanagement programming and metrics that have the potential for becoming less aligned with business strategies and less sensitive to the complexity of individual identities. In contrast, the broad-based approach is subject to vague lip service that employees cannot embrace because it may lack clarity with regard to workplace requirements.

A respect for differences, however defined, must rest with the understanding that organizations require different perspectives — regardless of their sources — and that these can be extensive. We advocate, however, that whichever approach is adopted by an organization, it must include the goal of acknowledging this breadth of differences (inclusiveness). To that end, we believe that these differences should be named and be relevant to the organization. The integration of intercultural competencies provides the answer as to how to do this.[2]

What is particularly relevant for our purposes is the understanding and recognition that values are drivers of behaviors. In general, values reflect general beliefs of what is right and wrong and what is generally preferable, or what "should be." Our attitudes can express our values and also dispose or predispose our actions and reactions, which in turn become our behaviors. Our biases, of course, are attitudes that may be driven by our values. To the extent that we can understand the fullest impact of our values and their worth, and perhaps their liabilities in some cases, organizations can educate their employees toward both inclusive attitudes and behaviors.

The dimensional characterizations commonly used to compare national cultures recognize the relationship between values and behaviors.[3] The dimensional constructs used for national cultural comparisons are useful in serving as a diving board of sorts into deeper waters. In life, people do not say, "I have uncertainty avoidance," or "I am a collectivist." Rather, they think and act in real terms. They have preferences for structure or certainty, or they act with their families' expectations in mind over what they might personally prefer to do. A cultural value approach can allow us to better understand our personal, interpersonal, and organizational interactions for the sake of managing our differences.

A strategy that follows the course of raising value-based questions can produce a picture of what "should be" for an organization and its people. For example, in the matter of social relationships, cultural constructs such as individualism and collectivism — which represent preferences for the self versus for others — need to be explored more deeply along the lines of individual performance or team/group performance expectations and corresponding value attachments. Such value orientations can enable us to understand diversity and along with it, matters of commonality and differences that go beyond the surface. Cultural training professionals often use the metaphor of an iceberg to describe culture, making the distinction between the observable "tip" as cultural practices and customs, and the under-the-surface part as the values and beliefs that influence those practices and customs. Thus, the value orientations approach offers us concrete explanations of understanding the invisible — what is beneath the above-water part of the iceberg — that relates to the visible. Defining diversity through value orientations as a strategy offers organizations the opportunity to strike a meaningful middle road between extreme categorizations of current diversity definitions and approaches, as described.

In closing here, one may ask, "What about individual differences?" We do acknowledge that a Transformational Diversity strategy can be inclusive of individual differences. Where we might differ from more traditional approaches is that what is specific to the individual needs to go beyond the uniqueness of personality and individual experiences to include the individual as the product of many historical, societal, and contextual influences — which are cultural, in our words. Hence, organizations have the responsibility to help their individual employees understand their personal orientations and preferences in relation to the needs of the organization. Certainly, many organizations do offer professional development programs such as self-assessment tools, coaching, and mentoring that allow for self-discovery and improvement. However, people need to enlarge their self-actualization activities to include the broader cultural influences on their personal makeup and their personal orientations toward work.

Dimensions of Consequence

A general strategy that focuses on what we term "dimensions of consequence" is one that understands cultural dimensional concepts and their corresponding values and links these to the work of the organization. In this regard, we agree with one of the key tenets of Andrés Tapia's recent work *The Inclusion Paradox* that "true diversity and inclusion requires calling out our differences, not minimizing them."[4] For us, this approach is a twofold effort — that of understanding differences and then linking them — that may take some true leadership, if not bravery. We have already pointed out how important it is for an organization to have a meaningful definition of diversity. This meaningfulness should be regularly updated to go hand in hand with the times. While diversity leaders may have difficulty ignoring established practices because the leaders are measured by how they follow these practices, they may need to assess the relevancy of their definitions or their organizational situations. In our view, diversity practitioners invoke an established or "best practice" list of dimensions of difference, yet smart leaders need to consider relevancy rather than imitation. They need to ask and answer the question of what are the dimensional differences of consequences to their people and business. The possibilities are considerable, such as conflicting attitudes about time or dramatically different communication styles, as we will shortly point out.

In sum, this strategy does not focus on assumed group identities or categorizations, which can be subject to reinforcing negative stereotyping. Nor does it focus on metrics. It is open to understanding the breadth of human possibilities. We can also accept individuals whose identities can be both independent of and dependent on others in their formation. In this way, an organization can demonstrate inclusion for its acceptance of the many bicultural and multicultural influences on today's workforce population.

Aligning Domestic Diversity to Global Diversity

Our final strategy is one of the main components of what we believe Transformational Diversity to be — that of a mindfulness of its potential linkage to and alignment with global workplace requirements. Cultural complexity and interactions continue to be the hallmarks of U.S. society with the third wave of immigration that began in the 1980s. Companies can continue to be solely domestic in their business and still need to deal with the workforce issues of diversity and multiculturalism. Other companies that have evolved in size and scope and even strategy to be considered international, multinational, or global in their composition and markets, of course, face the effects of cultural diversity each business day. Consequently, we would argue that the need for cultural competence is compelling for any organization, and especially if its business is still considered domestic. In today's age, fewer and fewer companies remain entirely domestic in their activities, and more organizations have increasing links to overseas or cross-border markets. While they may yet classify themselves as international businesses, we call them "pre-global" for our purposes. If cultural competency is developed early in an organization's global path, it can help accelerate success in matters involving international mergers, acquisitions, and even offshoring, among other growth strategies as they present themselves.

To be sure, the transformation of domestic diversity and a corresponding alignment require leadership that is culturally competent, representing an opportunity for domestic diversity professionals to undertake their own cultural competency-building agenda and lead others in this effort. Many of those who have long led domestic diversity programs have come from social activist backgrounds on behalf of specific constituencies, and we owe them much. Becoming culturally competent is no longer a skill requirement only for international HR professionals and expatriate populations. It is an essential requirement for doing business, especially for an organization's leaders. Without cultural competency, effectively communicating in respectful terms with subsidiaries or international business partners on any matter, much less on the subject of diversity, is not possible.

STRATEGY: STRESSING VALUES

Values Drive Behaviors

At a recent HR conference, a U.S.-born CEO of a global company told his audience that he did not believe in differences, because he claimed, "We all have the same plumbing." Upon hearing this remark, the audience let out a collective gasp.

No one should doubt that at the biological level we are all fundamentally alike. However, this CEO's view is not uncommon. Too many leaders do not want to deal with the difficulties of managing differences, so they commit their organizations only to diversity compliance requirements. In essence, they are not able to move beyond a common posture of universalism that assumes "we are all really alike." This posture, too, is not open to understanding what culture is and what its influences are. So from universalisms to denials, some leaders continue to lead without acknowledging the sources of differences and their implications for their organizations.

Fortunately, we believe the opinion of this CEO can be changed. An understanding of culture and its origins in value systems can enable leaders to recognize its application for organizations. Just as values drive the behaviors of individuals, the value-driven behaviors also underpin the behaviors of groups of people and of organizations, whether the source is recognized or not. Transformational Diversity requires work in all areas of focus: the individual employee, all groups of employees, and the organizational culture itself.

The Workplace as an Interdependent World

Despite all the focus on individualism in the U.S. culture and the individual ways that people differ, Transformational Diversity exists on the basic assumption that the workplace is an interdependent world. Most organizations claim to empower every employee to take responsibility for his or her career, yet increasingly both performance and progress are measured by group behaviors and outcomes. Certainly individual performance is often critical to the success of organizational breakthroughs and innovation. And engaging each employee as an individual in the organization is important. Nonetheless, we can no longer ignore the growing requirement for interdependence arising from the presence of pipelines of collaboration in today's increasingly competitive work environment. While the ability of people to work together on specific tasks, such as in departmental activities and teams or in reaching general business objectives and goals, may be long standing, working interdependently is now more crucial. We see interdependencies and intersections of job and functional activities in areas such as customer or client service, accelerated new product development and rush to market activities, operational and organizational changes for cost savings, and technology implementation and support to keep pace with communications and efficiencies. We can also see this interdependence in the increase of corporate surveys directed toward customer satisfaction and employee engagement. The message is clear to us that even survey feedback on performance (which we assume is appropriately valued) is another form of interdependence.

Transformational Diversity calls for a focus on understanding, recognizing, and rewarding *both* individual and group performances and the relationship between the two. In cultural terms, the relationship between the two is what matters in the workplace. This is not unlike what Nancy Adler advises on the subject of cross-cultural communication — that in any point of interaction or communication, we should assume difference until similarity is proven.[5] Anticipating conflicts and difficulties in interactions can pave the way toward positive outcomes and cooperation.

In the workplace, we recognize that most of our interactions come from teamwork, and the subject of teamwork has received much attention in business for many years for several reasons. First, teamwork is now understood to be the way to accomplish results most efficaciously, that is, if differences are managed. Second, teams, and especially global and virtual teams, are becoming more commonplace. A department or a business unit group constitutes a team, as does a temporary grouping of people for a specific project. Third, and most important, teamwork deserves attention because it is hard, and it is especially hard for U.S.-Americans who are acculturated to value their individual rather than team achievement. Despite clarion calls for team play and cohesion by team leaders (that are usually couched in sports terms), many U.S.-American employees still struggle with an instinct that says "I prefer to be a star player" instead.

If we doubt why teamwork is difficult in the U.S. environment, consider the following sample from some of the best sellers in popular business publications:

- *Getting More: How to Negotiate to Achieve Your Goals in the Real World* by Stuart Diamond (2010)

- *Winning* by Jack Welch (2007)

- *The Power of You! How YOU Can Create Happiness, Balance, and Wealth* by Scott Martineau (2006)

- *Brag!: The Art of Tooting Your Own Horn without Blowing It* by Peggy Clause (2003)

Winning and bragging are aspects of today's prevalent management theories and popular approaches that encourage individual achievement through assertive behaviors and self-belief. Although specific to the corporate workplace, such publications continue to reinforce the broader societal value placed on individualism in the United States. This alignment of values and their applications is not unusual; however, given the cultural diversity of today's workforce, self-interest over consideration of others can run counter to team behaviors and outcomes.

Teamwork as well as team leadership requires learned skill sets and behaviors. The development of these skill sets rests not only with management development professionals but also with diversity strategists and practitioners. Transformational Diversity suggests a refocused strategy that covers both individual and collective value differences in independent and interdependent terms as they play out in the entire workplace. We explain more about this strategy in the next section.

Bridging Collectivism with Individualism

Social scientist Harry C. Triandis believed that about 70 percent of the world's people could be found in collectivist or group-oriented cultures/societies.[6] While this statistic may be a wobbly estimate in today's global world, it is nonetheless an important one to consider in terms of diversity in the United States. Given the home countries and cultural sources of immigrants to the United States, we may need to recognize that increasingly our social and corporate environments are populated with people who are group oriented, or who are collectivists, not individualists. A traditional diversity strategy has been to apportion the workforce into affinity groupings, which would include larger ethnic/racial and immigrant groups. Many of our ethnic, and in some cases racial, groups share common values and orientation in support of the group rather than in support of the self. Yet in our diversity efforts we often fail to explore how we can better integrate this orientation or bridge the differences between the organization's expectations and those of employee groups, which can likely be a problem.

A strategy that supports understanding the value differences would have the benefit of recognizing the value in having employees with group orientations or preferences in their work styles. Among these benefits are considerations for harmony, for consensus, and for relationship-building. Some others benefits will be discussed as examples in the following section of working with differences of relevance.

Training can educate employees as to alternative orientations in positive terms. All employees could learn how to identify their own orientations — and to not be prejudged on the basis of where they were born or where others were born. Diversity strategies that call for this element can enable employees to understand their work-style orientations as strengths and the consequences of their culture-defined preferences for individual and interdependent group performance.

As a general strategy for diversity, however, valuing and linking alternative identity formation and behaviors, such as collectivism, suggests that the workplace could be transformed in positive ways. Of main interest to diversity practitioners is to empower employees who may be identified only by their ethnicity now to move into a place where they can bring added value to work productivity. If organized as an affinity group, they could share their perspectives and experiences with another affinity group and thereafter work together to share common perspectives with the larger employee community. These groups may also offer an entirely different perspective on practices such as relationship-building, expectations of leadership, and work/life balance issues, which if respected and welcomed could help make inclusion a reality.

STRATEGY: STRESSING DIFFERENCES OF RELEVANCE

As we mentioned in our introduction to Transformational Diversity strategy, we believe that organizations can transform their diversity commitments through a focus on differences of consequence or relevance. From a cultural framework, we offer a number of examples here, but they can be used more or less depending on the organization's business, corporate values, and employee composition. What you will notice is that they are not illustrative of traditional diversity categories for the most part. Rather, they are matters that affect everyone in an organization.

Communication Styles

From a cultural perspective, the matter of communication style is the preferred difference of relevance to start with.

Example. In a leading professional services organization with a robust program of traditional affinity group activities, a group of employees newly hired from a number of European countries felt excluded from some of the programs offered under the diversity and inclusion umbrella. They felt that they too represented a common group because of their adjustment needs and that they held a shared perspective of relevance to the organization. They all had a difficulty in understanding their U.S.-American managers' communication style. Consequently, they began to meet on their own within the context of various functional and internationally focused business groups to explore their exclusion. They developed their own learning programs around cultural adjustment to the U.S. work culture and placed an emphasis on communication differences. Fortunately for them, the organization was flexible enough to ultimately designate the group as a firm-supported diversity affinity group. In the process, the organization gained a learning program that could be reproduced in the locations having large numbers of international populations. Upper management also learned that some sensitivity in the use of language would make a big difference in communication circles.

The point. Although this example had a positive outcome, it should help us understand how we may miss commonalities among our employees that can provide value to the whole organization. This example also points to the changing composition of our workforce — many of whom require acculturation to the organization — regardless of how new they are to U.S. soil. Perhaps the following more interpersonal example will help clarify this issue.

Example. A recent female immigrant from South Asia (India) was working in an office late in the afternoon with a female project teammate from the United States. They held similar positions in their computer consulting company in New York. Each was working at her respective tasks, when the Indian woman remembered she had to leave early to pick up her son from school. She profusely and extensively explained to her colleague that she had to leave and apologized for any inconvenience. The U.S. employee, without looking up at her as she spoke, simply said, "It's ok with me. It is not like we are joined at the hip." The Indian woman then left promptly, feeling upset and confused by her colleague's response.

The point. This incident can replicate itself many times over between members of every team. The newcomer seeks to be extremely polite but perceives an abrupt, impolite response. Moreover, she has no idea what "joined at the hip" means or implies, and dislikes the image. She feels hurt and insulted. Likely, her colleague thinks nothing of the exchange at all, as she continued to stay focused on her task.

For the most part, organizations focus on communications as a matter of how many, rather than on the more important question of "how." For example, most of us understand that internal organization-wide communications are critical to employee engagement in many areas. Thus, decisions need to be made as to which media outlets to use, depending on the content, such as newsletters, intranets, and e-mails, and on how much content needs to be made known and when. In today's environment, other technology-based vehicles such as Facebook are often deployed for communication purposes. From a cultural perspective, however, certain formats (and along with these, certain patterns of expression) may create problems of misunderstanding and possibly feelings of exclusion by some employee audiences.

Intercultural research is very mature in terms of pointing out differences in the area of communications. It structures our perceptions in terms of understanding what is termed as "high" and "low context," that is, the matter of how much information to convey and what are the relationships and experiences that effect how one understands the message. The research also helps us understand how communication styles such as directness or vagueness influence our audiences' understanding.

Many organizations already practice a standard communications approach that places the responsibility for being understood on the sender of the communications. Yet, in intercultural situations, defined as situations where the sender and the receiver of the communications have culturally determined different styles of communicating (omitting the possibility of communicating in a second language), the responsibility may not be just the sender's. Misunderstandings are common in such situations. The U.S.-American corporate pattern of directness, coupled with excessive information (considered "low context" because nothing is assumed and everything needs to be verbalized or detailed), is often uncomfortable for some receivers of the information who are "high context" conditioned. High context means a need to have established social relationships and trust in place; hence, less detail is required. This approach is more commonly used by people from non-Anglo cultures. Not surprisingly, foreign-born employees of U.S. companies often complain about not understanding what their managers say when the latter use U.S. sports terms in group communications. Just what does "it's your turn to bat" mean to those without this shared knowledge or experience? Tasks may not be carried out if they are seemingly insensitive or out of context to the audience.

Alternative styles of communication are equally valid and can be found in many cultural environments around the world — and hence, among our employees. These would include less direct or indirect word choices, less explicit speech, more body language, and greater personal relationship-building in advance, before someone as a receiver might take action. If an organization deems directness important, with consequent body language that calls for "looking someone in the eye" so that the sender receives feedback that the message has been understood, we suggest that this value is of consequence to the organization. At the same time, since alternative possibilities can and do exist among employees, we also suggest that leadership has the responsibility to point out these differences and to train everyone to understand, accept, and work well with all communication styles. Training and development along the lines of developing alternative or different styles of communication do exist and can be offered. For example, the U.S. style of directness and confrontation, which so often go together, could be explored from the opposite perspective so that others who may prefer less direct communication can remain equally committed to a task. Therefore, diversity training in communication needs to demonstrate possible conflicts in, as well as the preferred aspects of, communication to avoid misunderstandings.

Relationship-Building

A second area of differences for many organizations is that of understanding the role of relationships. This understanding is especially important between leaders and teams or groups, and between members of teams or groups. Especially obvious in matters between team members and their supervisors, some people feel more comfortable in preexisting developed relationships, and they perform better accordingly. Other issues, such as distance and time, may impede anyone in relationship-building, and the very presence of these issues often affects individual performance and productivity. If an organization values its collaborative culture, or integrity and relationships in its customer service, relationship-building may be extremely critical to its survival. Some cultures may favor relationships over rules in their hierarchy of personal values. Relationship-building is not a matter for easy simplification but rather a subject for considerable learning and importance.

Time

Time as a concept can be considered as another value of consequence in diversity management strategy. The Western and U.S. focus on time is to value it tangibly, like a commodity. It is not to be wasted. Indeed, a "stitch in time . . ." is still a standard U.S. proverb. In the U.S. work environment, deadlines are set, and agendas are designed to be kept. Meetings, too, are expected to begin promptly. This time orientation, often labeled as short term and monochronic by social scientists, meaning focusing on one thing at a time, reflects a need for control, and it is not universally shared.

Despite globalization, time's importance as a short-term, tangible matter in doing business with and within a U.S. company does not appear to be lessening. Yet, many new immigrants to the United States bring with them a different sense of time consciousness. As a result, organizations need to ensure that time is valued in a common way that respects employees' desire for relationship-building and their preferred communication styles. Consider for a moment the question a manager might face with a new team composed of diverse members under a tight deadline. How much time should be devoted to team-building versus to getting the job done? The answers we might find are not so obvious and could be challenging. If some members feel uncomfortable because they do not know or understand each other, progress might be slow. On the other hand, if the team spends time getting to know each other, work may not progress fast enough. We would suggest that an understanding of the different perspectives in the first place may ease this challenge.

Gender Roles

The consideration of gender roles has long been included in diversity strategies as a dimension of categorical importance. We would argue that the values behind this dimension that can drive role expectations are more significant than any quantifiable or metric analysis as to the presence of women, in particular, in an organization.

As diversity practitioners in the United States begin to look to their few-and-far-between global counterparts for support, they may find the issue of gender and the role of women to be the one dimension of difference that can be agreed on. This commonality is understandable for many reasons. For the most part, because of the many economic changes resulting from globalization, more women are being educated and are entering the modern workforce at accelerated rates as compared to the past. (Readers can find considerable evidence of this development through available national country statistics and international labor data.)

The entrance of greater numbers of women into the workforce means that women are entering fields and roles previously considered to be male domains and are knocking at the doors of managerial positions within their organizations. Although successes have occurred in recent years, in too many places the doors have remained closed, and the "glass ceiling" has remained intact. Exploring issues of bias against women is a legitimate focus, as is exploring its origins, particularly in certain cultures or societies. But with the overall shortage of talent, qualified individuals cannot be overlooked regardless of gender. Consequently, what may have once been a moral case for women's inclusion is now a business imperative.

The evolution of the business case for the advancement and retention of women has produced some significant commitments from organizations to include this objective in their broader talent management strategies and programs, especially in organizations that employ a good number of women who represent irreplaceable talent. This situation also exists for organizations that must retain their very best people, regardless of gender, and for which the loss of top female talent would indicate less supportive corporate cultures. We note that, in some instances, this actuality can lead to a segregation of activities away from the diversity and inclusion function, and we do not believe that this somewhat independent or parallel course of action is satisfactory. Exploring gender roles needs to be coordinated and synergized with the organization's diversity commitments and activities.

Irrespective of organizational structures, however, there is much to consider along the lines of culture's impact on the roles of men and women in societies that can help strategic planners. Whether or not an organization commits to the role of women as a dimension of difference in talent management or in diversity and inclusion programs, seemingly little attention has been given to the larger societal and cultural contexts that may impact performances based on gender roles.

From an intercultural perspective, we suggest that some of the themes attached to Geert Hofstede's distinction between masculine- and feminine-oriented cultures offer some compelling insights into understanding the differences between gender styles.[7] In brief, he characterized masculine cultures as demonstrating orientations toward assertiveness, self-promotion, and competition, contrasted with cultures that have more "feminine" values such as cooperation and empathy. Current research on the issue of women in business supports a difference in management styles between men and women similar to Hofstede's descriptions. Within a multicultural workforce, male employees, depending on their cultures of origin (or cultural heritages), may exhibit more "feminine" characteristics than expected. A diversity strategy that acknowledges and accepts these differences, regardless of gender, as being equally important to the way business is conducted can be a transformative one. We close this discussion about gender roles with the following example of a personal cross-cultural experience.

Example: A group of South Korean female national legislators conducted a study visit to the United States to explore models in governmental and corporate arenas that focused on advancing women. In meeting with corporate representatives in one firm with a notable women's advancement program, the visitors expressed their surprise in learning that corporate commitment to the issue seemed independent of government social-engineering policies, such as they hoped they might implement at home. They stated that they were also surprised to learn that U.S. women were still earning less than their male counterparts and that more work in women's advancement had yet to be done.

The point. In debriefing this example, the exchange quite naturally caused members of each group to comment on the difference between the U.S. and South Korean cultures in managing change on behalf of women. However, both parties did not discuss and missed the opportunity to explore some of the same underlying causes of discrimination existing in both of their societies that could not be changed either through legislation or through women-friendly programs, namely culture-embedded "masculine" values. We suggest that future participants in such a dialogue could learn about bridging commonalities as much as differences.

Recruitment and Beyond

We have titled this section simply "Recruitment and Beyond" to suggest that organizations need to create their own issues of consequence to transform their diversity strategies to lead them in raising productivity and performance. Recruiting programs that target minorities, or racial/ethnic-based populations presently underrepresented in the organization, have a long history and a rightful one in most instances. For many organizations, a targeted recruitment program may be the only aspect of their diversity activities, and as such, it constitutes a baseline for diversity programs in that it has a strong aspect of legal compliance attached to it. Nonetheless, this representational approach without further focus on the differences of relevance made by the target populations, and made possible by education and training, can be an unsuccessful process, and a dangerous one. The newly hired may fail or remain isolated in the organization, and anti-affirmative action mindsets can be reinforced. Seen from another viewpoint, we may need to consider that ethnic-based recruitment policies may overemphasize differences, exaggerate categorizations, and in general work against the intercultural and multicultural attributes found among our employee base.[8] Similarly, target recruitment efforts may affect an organization's overall diversity program by causing it to lose momentum and support, not to mention some of its recruitment brand.

Among the other possibilities are the values arising from religious beliefs and social class, both of which can produce social divisions. Generational differences, too, may be consequential. Studies on the characteristics of the current coming-of-age generation, the Millennials, and others are available, for example, by the Pew Research Center and can help human resources understand relevant differences in how people engage with each other and their organizations. Considering these generational differences may take courage, but that is one of the features of the Transformational Diversity strategy.

Example. A top-tier international law firm, headquartered in the United States, had a successful diversity program that was based only on recruiting black employees. It found that everyone, including the new recruits, was having difficulty with many of their new immigrant clients in terms of communication, thinking processes, and attitudes toward risk. Then, an expanded diversity program that centered on understanding cultural differences along these lines was implemented by driving the international experience of the organization toward the domestic marketplace. In time, the local diversity program expanded to include this training as mandatory for the domestic market, to everyone's benefit.

The point. Having a more robust and proactive diversity program that went beyond recruitment to include expanding the skill sets and knowledge of all employees could have added to the firm's capability to serve its clients and increased its profitability.

STRATEGY: ALIGNING DOMESTIC DIVERSITY TO GLOBAL

We have previously introduced our reasoning as to why Transformational Diversity calls for revising domestic diversity strategy and program mindsets in the direction of global developments. We mentioned the ever-expanding cultural diversity and complexities of the U.S. workforce and the need for all organizations to be globally prepared, such as through intercultural business competencies that play into teambuilding and raised productivity. We now turn to expanding our business case on this strategy by first pointing to the context of the broader U.S. and global diversity environments, and then by addressing issues of organizational change in diversity matters.

Contexts

The USA: Pluralism and Multiculturalism. A recent U.S. government report entitled, Building an Americanization Movement for the Twenty-first Century, found that the workplace is where immigrants to the United States feel the most acclimated culturally. The report states, "In many ways, the journey toward integration begins at the workplace."[9]

Example. A female department head in a major university, once a new immigrant from India, claimed privately that her rise up the ladder began only when she stopped wearing a sari and started wearing Western clothes.

The point. In this instance, an individual made a change in favor of assimilation, at least in the overt sense, and it made a difference to her in her career.

The topic of assimilation has become more controversial in recent years than ever before. Some groups argue in favor of preserving and celebrating various ethnic identities, which corresponds to what social theorists deem to be the "solidarity model." Others, in contrast, favor a less separatist approach, favoring a "unified model." This model strives to include people of more than one racial/ethnic or cultural group so that there are evidences of both or more groups to be found in new practices or behaviors. Both models have their place in various descriptions of U.S. pluralism, yet the latter is more focused on multiculturalism as a goal. Both models assume assimilation to U.S. culture in due course, but the latter looks to accepting a changed culture for the future.

We will make no attempt here to enter this polemic as to social, educational, and even political policy requirements affecting the new immigrants in the United States. Certainly, one can argue that the U.S. government, by sponsoring the aforementioned study, is playing a fitting role by encouraging and assisting immigrants in joining U.S. society and civil life as soon as possible. Corporations, on the other hand, make no such assumptions about assimilation or take on this role directly. The issue, of course, is that they do so indirectly. Intriguingly, given corporate buy-in in the United States on the matter of diversity, few corporate voices can be heard in the public arena on this discussion. As mentioned in Chapter 3, now may be the time for corporate leadership to speak up and not to remain silent. In light of the recent example of the challenge made to Judge Sonia Sotomayor during her confirmation hearings for the U.S. Supreme Court, that she might be "too empathetic" as a Latina, one wonders if that sort of comment would be allowed in a corporate work team that comprised multicultural members.

The history of diversity management in the corporate United States suggests that both the models of solidarity and multiculturalism apply and seem to mirror the current public dilemma as to which path to take to integration. Organizational diversity programs still take on the preservation of ethnic distinctions and customs through affinity groups, but they can fail to integrate (or include) corresponding cultural orientations held by representatives from these groups in the workplace. In these instances, they take on the language of inclusion similar to the unified model, while behaving otherwise.

For our purposes here, however, we believe that the evolutionary U.S. environment, or context, affects our employees and their expectations, and therefore, it can be relevant to their employers. If, as the aforementioned report indicates, U.S. immigrants as employees report that the workplace is the place where they feel "American," this feeling reflects some sense of change in their identities or in their ability to manage biculturally or multiculturally. Just as the Indian academic mentioned in our example made the decision to adjust for herself, she was allowed to do so. Possibly, others in similar situations may not feel as comfortable in becoming more westernized or corporate.

The challenge for corporations is then to accept these employees' self-perceptions, which can be fluid and changing, rather than to define perceptions for them. Richard Lewis draws attention to the fact that some cultures have "black holes."[10] These are very deep, and an awareness of them as areas where change could be difficult will at least need to be considered in meeting this challenge. Here again is an area where intercultural competency or a global mindset is helpful.

Similarly, organizations need to recognize that employees of various ethnic, racial, and cultural heritages do not necessarily self-identify categorically or are comfortable with such categorizations. In both instances, for employees who actively engage in their cultural or racial identities and for employees who do not, a danger of perpetuating stereotypes rather than of preventing them exists. We do acknowledge that diversity programming has demonstrated to date a rightful focus on educating employees on what constitutes bias and stereotyping in behaviors, but perhaps more needs to be explored organizationally.

Leaders, in particular, need to be further trained to identify culture conflicts of the social identity type. They and their organizations need to recognize that not every conflict nowadays in the United States is a matter of pure and simple interpersonal disagreement. Preventing culture-embedded conflicts by educating employees directly benefits teamwork, productivity, and performance.

Global. The global context is for many reasons as relevant for all HR professionals, domestic and international, as it is for the leaders of global organizations. We have previously discussed issues of managing a diverse U.S. workforce due to immigration. The challenge of immigration to management is not just a U.S. phenomenon. HR colleagues in many countries, especially in Europe, are also facing this challenge. Serious demographic changes are likewise global, especially large aging populations. Consequently, issues of an aging workforce and related costs present a domestic challenge for companies and governments everywhere. Most important to our thinking, however, regarding the global context is the matter of globalization itself and the controversy surrounding its effect on the convergence of cultures. This matter is often referred to as the convergence or divergence issue.

Cultural preservationists decry what they perceive to be the convergence of many economic and social practices that in many countries are caused by global corporate behavior, among other things. The media and technology are also mentioned as causes. As organizations grow globally or seek to be global companies, they need to standardize, coordinate, and be consistent in their practices and policies without any cultural bias. Local cultural differences, however, continue to arise and often challenge these goals. Sometimes these differences escalate into failures of local implementation of global practices. Sometimes these differences are so imbedded that mergers fall apart, for example, the Daimler Chrysler case. What is relevant to us here is that both the conventional wisdom and literature on global organizations call for global integration with local responsiveness. This balancing act between consistency of approaches, a common corporate culture, and adaptation by local subsidiaries for the local markets is a tall order.

As Thomas Friedman reminds us, the tension between what the Lexus and the olive tree represent in his notable book is part and parcel of globalization.[11] The modern world of English as the global language of communication, the shared use of the Internet and other technologies, and the ever-growing integration of economies, as represented by the Lexus automobile, daily confront and affront people's sense of identities and roots, as symbolized by an olive tree. Quite simply, the challenge that organizational leaders face in balancing between these ends closely parallels, in our view, our domestic diversity environments. Skills and competencies are required to manage a delicate balance not only across continents and cultures but also across our corporate hallways.

Organizational Change. Aligning domestic diversity activities to an organization's global developments opens up a number of special considerations in managing organizational change. Among them are the understanding of the global growth processes and the nature of global corporate cultures; the history of issues surrounding past efforts at working globally with models reflecting typical U.S. diversity approaches; the need for new skills and competencies in general; and last, the professional competencies of HR business leaders as navigators for this change.

Socialization and Standardization

To manage organizational change that aligns domestic to global diversity, the diversity leaders require the same competencies as do their business leaders. As previously mentioned they must understand the global requirements of standardization and consistency and balance these with local adaptation or localization. The ability to actually carry out the strategies that call for this balance where necessary can come from cultural awareness or, in other words, intercultural sensitivity. Cultural awareness (or intercultural sensitivity) is defined as understanding one's own organizational culture in terms of its values, attitudes, and preferences. It is the starting point for anticipating differences of consequence among a company's global partners or subsidiaries. Moreover, it helps organizations understand the strength of its cultural positioning and to learn how to adjust for changes as required when working globally. In this way, appropriate and successful socialization by new employees and business partners to the organization can be made possible.

Exporting U.S. Diversity Programs

A decade ago, during globalization strategy discussions, we experienced a gathering of some 400 people from 25 countries in a series of focus groupings to discuss the exploration of their shared values. The intent was to reach consensus on one of these, "Respect for Diversity." The topic generated considerable discussion because, other than those participants from the United States, few people at the meetings understood its meaning. When the time came to reach a decision, since people from outside the United States comprised the majority, the resulting global value was adopted as "Respect for Cultural Diversity."

This reaction was more than nuanced. To many participants from outside the United States the concept of diversity was strange, and possibly "dangerous," in part, as described by George Simons.[12] The concept was dangerous because, within the European context and history in particular, some aspects of diversity management such as "celebrating differences" are considered too provocative, if not politically difficult. On the other hand, as Simons points out, cultural diversity was viewed as the starting point for managing differences, rather than the end point of the diversity. Cultural diversity was generally considered to be more relevant in non-U.S. environments than "diversity" itself, based on past experiences, current realities, and the future. The matter was not one of redressing past discriminations but instead of moving forward in better ways than in the past.

Beyond this example, there is now a substantial history and discussion about some of the experiences of U.S. companies in their efforts to develop, or rather to extend, their U.S. successes in diversity management to the global scene. This history, however, has been difficult, and it provides us with a limited number of best practices in global diversity to date, for two important reasons. The first is that the U.S.-American diversity experience is unique; the second is the influence of a general

U.S.-American cultural orientation toward universalism, or a belief that only one single principle should be applied to all situations.

While every society has its unique history, the U.S. history has coupled its immigration-based roots with values of social equality and upward mobility, sometimes referred to as "the American dream." Elements of past U.S. experiences that include race relations produced legal and moral mandates that are at the root of U.S. diversity programs. As we saw with the aforementioned discussions between U.S. and European counterparts on the issue of diversity, these experiences are not easily shared. Diversity receptivity among countries is a cultural difference of some consequence. North America has the largest percentage of foreign-born populations compared to other regions, according to UNESCO.[13] It also has the fewest number of official languages (two versus the double digits found in many other regions), which allows for ease of communication between different groups in all areas of common life. Thus, the idea of the American dream is sustainable, given the higher degree of assimilation by U.S. immigrants.

The second issue, that of the U.S. cultural orientation toward universalism, is more pronounced in how U.S.-Americans do business. Policies, manuals, and sets of standards are common practice exemplifying universalism. As recently discussed at length by global cultural consultants,[14] this belief in the application of "but one best way" conflicts with those cultures whose members value their relationships and distinctiveness instead, referred to as "particularism."[15] Universalism is often accompanied by a sense of rightness in the case of diversity discussions. As long as universalism and its corresponding behaviors and attitudes prevail, this U.S.-American cultural orientation will continue to inhibit our country's global collaboration, and global diversity will remain problematic.

If diversity professionals remain challenged to support global efforts, they can begin by being flexible and elastic in their strategies to allow for local adaptation. The template for activities that are widely used in the United States (including affinity groups and national- and ethic-based data, among other things) cannot be forced. In fact, the data privacy laws in many countries make gathering data difficult, so many global companies are already learning to do without this level of detail. We suggest, therefore, that when beginning to plan for expanding into the global arena, U.S. diversity managers may need to consider first what may not work — such as data-gathering and detail on ethnic or racial makeup — before considering what may work. Here again, an understanding of cultural contexts may help them start by pointing to issues of difference as well as to issues of commonality.

New Skills and Competencies

We deliberately included throughout our discussions of strategy some comment on the need for diversity practitioners to develop their abilities in understanding culture and in being culturally sensitive in practice. Cultural competencies that stress cultural awareness, the ability to engage in cultural dialogs to elicit information and to adjust one's behaviors appropriately, should be included in the professional development of domestic diversity professionals, as they are for global HR professionals. To be a business change partner in global developments takes the ability to help navigate the organization globally. It takes insight into the perspective of others to anticipate problems or differences of opinions and customs. How can one have a discussion about inclusion with people from countries that may have histories of not being receptive to diversity or that may be defined as monocultures? If a company decides to off-shore its payroll to Bangalore, it needs to have internal HR professionals capable of addressing differences in management styles between U.S.-Americans, or headquarters employees, and the Indian staff in India, so that differences can be managed before problems arise.

Expanding HR Roles

While human resources has always had a role in getting the basics right in terms of internal processes and operational administration for people for an organization, it also needs to expand its responsibility in the direction of building capacity for the organization to be competitive and more profitable. Intercultural training and education programs can support building that capacity in addition to achieving diversity and inclusion objectives. Such training will also expand human resources' role in helping the organization tackle the challenge of balancing standardization with localization as the organization grows internationally.

The context of the expansion of HR roles in today's marketplace also represents an opportunity for self-development by HR professionals. A strategic commitment to transforming diversity in the direction of intercultural integration represents a learning and growth opportunity that is no longer a luxury in today's environment.

STRATEGY: ORGANIZATION-WIDE DEVELOPMENT OF INTERCULTURAL SENSITIVITY

Organizational change in the direction of expanded intercultural awareness and sensitivity, along with inclusive behaviors, takes time. It cannot be accomplished overnight even with the best of commitments, resources, and implementation plans. No wonder, then, that if we add the time factor to the lack of understanding the business case, culture change in the direction of intercultural sensitivity is not receiving attention. As with individual changes in intercultural awareness, understanding what change looks like and how to begin is helpful. For this reason we favor understanding change in developmental terms so that behaviors are identifiable, problems are understood, progress can be measured, and goals can be achieved.

A simple but thorough picture of a development approach was developed by Dr. Milton J. Bennett in the 1980s and expanded in 1993 (see Appendix A for a brief summary of the Development Model for Intercultural Sensitivity, or DMIS). In brief, he described two broad phases or stages, the "from" and "to," with corresponding sub phases and attributes to explain how we can move from experiencing our own culture as the central reality to constructing and accepting a reality that is more reflective and integrating of other cultures. Bennett's model was intended for individual and group audiences, such as expatriates and immigrants, needing to adapt to and understand new cultures, but he, along with Janet Bennett, expanded its use later to the challenge of providing global training on the subject of diversity.[16] To its credit, the strength of DMIS lies in recognizing that accepting "differences" was a matter of experiences (not just knowledge), which he describes as phased changes in the direction of new but accepting attitudes and behaviors or international sensitivity.

The process of organizational change in the direction of intercultural sensitivity, unfortunately, does not always produce incremental and positive results without organizational self-awareness. A similar development model of organizational change is available through "Global Diversity and Inclusion Benchmarks" as an assessment tool.[17] As its name suggests, the work draws upon established diversity benchmarks and breaks these down in progressive terms with appropriate descriptions. Any ability to self-assess organizationally along a positive trajectory by using perhaps a model that identifies the particulars of each phase such as Milton Bennett's, or comparable best practices along the way as with the mentioned tool, can make transformation happen.

In summary, by recognizing the possibility of naming an organization's developmental stages, diversity leadership can determine areas where the organization is "stuck" versus areas to where it should go next. In addition, diversity leadership can recognize when the organization is progressing for measurement purposes. We need to move beyond the numbers, from standard metrics that quantify changes based on representation only, to an ability to include qualitative changes within an organization. While an organization identifying its leadership board, for example, on the basis of representation of different ethnicities, races, and gender may be meaningful, in the absence of qualitative examples, a perception of "tokenism" may stay attached to this practice. Even where representation measures are well regarded and working (and not suspect), an ability to add qualitative identifiers to an organization's diversity practices will represent action that characterizes intercultural sensitivity.

FRAMEWORK: AREAS OF TRANSFORMATIONAL DIVERSITY INTERVENTION

Our understanding of the workplace as an interdependent environment and the complexity of any organization's structures and functions suggest that not many aspects of the organization go untouched by matters of diversity. Consequently, diversity management calls for an integrated organization-wide approach. Diversity departments and their activities should not just sit as "other" or as a subset of the HR function, independent from other activities. Diversity and inclusion vision needs to be positioned as a driver of corporate cultural change that values diversity for business reasons and for efficient talent management. Figure 4.1 is offered to suggest how diversity in general, and Transformational Diversity as a vision in particular, touches the many business and HR department activities of an organization.

Whether housed in human resources or as a standalone function, perhaps reporting to senior management directly, diversity and inclu-

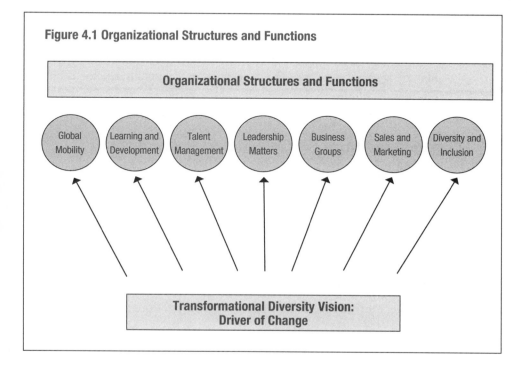

Figure 4.1 Organizational Structures and Functions

Organizational Structures and Functions

Global Mobility | Learning and Development | Talent Management | Leadership Matters | Business Groups | Sales and Marketing | Diversity and Inclusion

Transformational Diversity Vision: Driver of Change

sion leadership is responsible for the whole organization. For diversity to succeed, the diversity and inclusion commitments of an organization must apply to all that it does, and to its total employee population. Change on behalf of inclusion does not only "trickle down" from leadership examples; it also needs to "trickle up" from the different perspectives and experiences of employees. It needs to take place within any grouping of people, such as with department work units or project teams. For this reason, diversity leaders have any number of possible areas for intervening for effective and transformative change. They need only to begin.

WHERE TO BEGIN TRANSFORMATIONAL DIVERSITY

We will introduce a number of program examples as implementation steps in the next chapter. For now, however, we offer some suggestions for strategic planning purposes centering on the following:

- The principle of engaging all levels and groups of employees

- The integration of traditional affinity group objectives and activities to help drive cultural change within the organization; our focus on affinity groups in this regard is based on the recognition that so many organizations use affinity groups as a benchmark for their diversity programming

Engagement Must Be Considered at All Levels

Onboarding. New employee orientations, sometimes referred to as onboarding, can be expanded beyond basic practices and policies of the organization to include information on the organization's cultural goals and makeup. General cultural awareness programming should begin at this time to deliver the messages of corporate commitments to diversity and inclusion and to ensure early socialization as to the expected behaviors. Content should be focused on understanding definitions of culture, race, ethnicity, stereotyping, and generalizations.

Global preparedness. First, diversity leadership should sponsor training that focuses on an understanding of globalization and on the organization's international business, including its global strategy, even if incipient. For global companies, global preparedness needs to be a basic knowledge and skill set for all its employees in order for them to do their business.

Second, since many global companies that value international competencies often hire individuals who speak a number of languages and who may already have international backgrounds and experiences, diversity management needs to leverage these individuals. Through the possibility of utilizing existing resources and incorporating them in various training and learning programs, such as understanding the U.S. as a multicultural environment, organizations can expand their collective global mindsets and skill sets. Certainly, a learning commitment along these lines, which draws upon mirroring employee interactions in the domestic workplace, can prepare employees for the real global marketplace. In this way, too, global competitive advantage is acquired.

Self-Assessments (Individual and Organizational)

Any intent to implement change requires assessments as to where one stands. Strategy, in particular, requires an analysis of internal and external factors applicable to the business. For HR practitioners, this strategy development also requires an assessment of both hard and soft elements (for example, technology systems and employee skill sets). Diversity leadership needs to ensure that the intercultural competencies of its employees, as well as the whole organization, need to be part of that assessment process. Oftentimes, we find an organization's diversity commitments within corporate websites in the "Careers" tab only. The intercultural competence of the organization and its commitments to diversity need to be positioned in other places such as in its corporate mission as well as in the current strategy goals. How to accomplish these objectives may well rest, we believe, on diversity leadership that understands its current strengths and weaknesses in these areas, which is after all a starting point for further strategy development.

Affinity Groups

Affinity groups, or employee networks, on an organized basis have existed within organizations of considerable size for many decades. Generally, these groups have served to eliminate discrimination, helping employees of common background in terms of race, ethnicity, or minority status such as sexual orientation to be successful in the organization. These groups have been successful to the extent employees wanted to self-identify categorically speaking and to participate in discussions and events for their own benefit and that of the organization. Within many organizations, however, affinity network activities have gravitated toward celebratory and social outcomes. Their real value, we believe, is to make known any differences represented by the individuals within the groups so that the differences can be respected, and thus, accepted, especially if they are not standard across the whole of the organization. This process is easier said than done. Rather than miss the opportunity for success, we turn to offering some suggestions for making this possible using our Transformational Diversity strategies.

We start with a basic premise that support for affinity groups should rest on a business case. Whether or not an organization provides the time, budgets, resources, and opportunities for the affinity groups to run, its memberships need to be accountable. Although voluntary, they need to have their own mission statements, guidelines, and goals. These, of course, can include identification of coaching and learning needs for the individuals. Their business contributions, however, need to be expected in return.

Affinity groups should be both sharing and learning focused. The interdependency we addressed earlier of how people work in an organization requires a two-way flow of learning. Differences in various work orientations that may stem from common histories and ethnicities need to be shared with others during culture-specific training. Intercultural competency requires that we be able to at least objectively discuss these differences led by an appropriate moderator. Diversity and inclusion call for a belief that differences of opinions and thought enhance organizational creativity and innovation. We need not squander the opportunities for dialogue that affinity groups represent. Intercultural training can and should be offered to affinity group participants so that they can first self-assess the strengths of their (cultural) orientations and then learn how to communicate and apply their strengths to enhance overall productivity, synergy, and performance.

Lastly, we offer a thought in consideration of the limits of affinity groups (or networks) as an effective diversity and inclusion strategy. To be truly transformative, we must consider this possibility too. Organizations need to create opportunities for their employees to explore the possibility of their various cultural identities and orientations. If we continue to insist that Hispanic American employees need to organize, are we not just patterning stereotypes? Yes, we are — to a certain extent. Of course, some employee groupings by national origins may be successful in broad terms if considerable cultural commonalities exist. A case in point may be Asian Americans. This group is diverse culturally, given the number of Asian countries, and experientially, ranging from second-generation immigrants to newly arrived international students. They face varying degrees of cultural change, and not all of them self-identify as being bicultural, as is the case of some Asian Americans, as pointed out by Jane Hyun.[18] We need to train our employees to be culturally self-aware, rather than make assumptions that they will somehow learn by themselves. We also suggest that intercultural knowledge and sensitivity can help the organization allow for sharing between and among affinity networks, for the betterment of the organization and the individuals involved, a topic that to date remains unexplored.

Having thus considered both general and specific strategies for implementing Transformational Diversity, as well as having provided some structure to the issue of where to begin implementing, we now turn the corner toward implementation.

Chapter 5. The *How* of Transformational Diversity

This chapter will show that Transformational Diversity is not just another diversity theory but an implementable vision and a very pragmatic doable approach. In the past chapters describing its business case and components, we laid down the basics as a road map. We now approach the most important venture in our journey, that of the practical How of Transformational Diversity. Thus we will discuss logistics by suggesting some proven — and customizable — action tools for implementation, which we put forth as a set of Transformational Diversity Action Archetypes.

Below, we point out the necessity of making a sustained effort in taking action for Transformational Diversity developments and present an outline for implementation based on our experiences. A discussion of the specifics of Transformational Diversity Action Archetypes as different from the traditional understanding of "archetype" is our first response to the How. Then we will address the strategies outlined in the What: each strategy will be matched with one or more Transformational Diversity application or Action Archetypes (the six of them making a toolbox for Transformational Diversity implementation.) Finally, we discuss Transformational Diversity benefits, as well as the attributes necessary for Transformational Diversity to move ahead, including awareness of a paradigm shift, agents of change, and suggested funding sources. We will also share some practical examples and considerations of the rollout that may be helpful for corporate human resources and intercultural consultants alike.

FINALIZING A ROAD MAP

While the How had been originally conceptualized as representing "to what extent" Transformational Diversity can be implemented, it does not present recipes for success, for a number of reasons. First and foremost, the total optimal implementation experiences for a new concept present a *contradictio in adjecto* (Latin for "contradiction in itself" or "contradiction in terms"): any number of accumulated experiences cannot be considered optimal or final for such a complex, ever-evolving new concept and practice as Transformational Diversity. Second, in its early stage of development, the experiences of rolling out Transformational Diversity initiatives are still fragmented and do not yet give us a full range of possible tools. Simply put, the ideally perfect description of experiences — and a perfect road map — cannot be possible in principle because Transformational Diversity is ever-developing, and by definition, is a vision calling for a major shift of focus in diversity developments, a shift from "old" diversity programming to inclusion, which is achieved by an increasingly potent infusion of intercultural business competencies into diversity practices across the board. This stated, the How is still a critical component of the road map to Transformational Diversity: it shows what kind of Action Archetypes proved most effective to date. Consequently, we have enough data to identify the mechanism that will take defined shape when customized at each participating organization. Thus, in this chapter we speak of the breadth of possibilities or the choices available today in classroom, virtual, and online training. Nothing is set in stone in Transformational Diversity; however, we hope that our road map helps lead our readers to open up their minds to new possibilities to transform diversity through our vision, strategies, and the tools/applications to be described.

TRANSFORMATIONAL DIVERSITY ACTION ARCHETYPES AS A TOOLBOX

Action Archetypes for Implementation

First, what are the Archetypes? "Archetype" is a bit of a buzzword in training and diversity circles right now. Although psychologist Carl Jung most influenced the modern understanding of the ancient concept of archetype, the term "archetype" was not actively used until later. Archetype is typically defined as the first original model of which all other objects, images, or concepts are derived, patterned, or emulated. In other words, the archetype for us is a generic model, an ideal example upon which we can build. This approach has been enormously popular and practically fruitful. The idea of using archetypes as models for cultural-diversity training is not altogether new; see, for instance, the article in *Business Communication Quarterly*.[1] We, however, are using archetypes for much broader goals, in part for presenting a big picture of Transformational Diversity training applications in a consistent manner, systematizing our perceptions and experiences of how Transformational Diversity implementation needs to be done. For this reason, we call them Action Archetypes.

How can we tell the difference between Action Archetypes and archetypes? An Action Archetype is not any static, inborn, ideal image or concept only. Instead, it is a "moveable feast" representing ever-evolving action, reflecting its inherently dynamic character. In an effort to present this variation in a succinct way we organized the related specifications in Table 5.1.

Each Action Archetype will illuminate core program series structure and content. Action Archetypes will also help you clearly see where

Table 5.1: Archetypes and Transformational Diversity Action Archetypes

Archetype	Action Archetype
Features	
Static nature	**Dynamic nature**
An ideal model/concept of which other concepts/objects are derivative	An action guide presenting the deep background structure of Transformational Diversity training session(s) and providing motivation and core meaning
	A prototype action upon which we build up and customize as needed
	It illuminates core program series structure and content
	It helps to clearly see where the diversity needs of organization may sit and what actions meet them
Applications	
Myers-Briggs Indicator (for establishing accurate personality profiling)	Transformational Diversity toolbox (for prioritizing aspects of Transformational Diversity projects, identifying needs and areas of special interest and then matching them with Transformational Diversity actions—in terms of participants, content, methodology, format, etc.)
Psychometric testing (for assessing suitability of candidates for employment)	Your actions: Decide which Transformational Diversity strategy makes the best fit for your needs and Select matching Action Archetype for implementation
Comparisons	
Archetype is like an idea of a certain meal and how it should be: *appetizer*, or *second course*, or *dessert*, etc.	Action Archetype is like an action guide of how to cook certain meals in the Transformational Diversity cuisine style. You learn how to meet the needs of your population satisfying their appetite for: fish or meat (content); raw or well-done (methodology); hot or mild (e-learning or classroom); fast-food or exquisite (format), etc. So, with Action Archetype you are your own Chef!

the diversity needs in your organization may reside and what type of target programs can meet these needs.

Action Archetypes Inventory

Thus, with the help of Action Archetypes you will have a strong tool for assessing the Transformational Diversity learning structure and for clarifying and testing programs, as well as for compiling many details involved in selecting the right program — the task that can prove overwhelming especially at the beginning of Transformational Diversity projects. Using Action Archetypes simplifies the process of looking at your Transformational Diversity programming while adding structure and a sense of direction to unrolling Transformational Diversity projects at organizations.

Let us now look at our Transformational Diversity Action Archetypes toolbox. Its dominant Action Archetypes will be described one after another as we address how to implement four Transformational Diversity strategies, and you will see that some of them can hold "dual citizenship," that is, serve more than one strategy need. Our Action Archetypes are as follows:

1. Action Archetype I, America the Diverse™
2. Action Archetype II, Communicating Across Cultures
3. Action Archetype III, Diversity Coaching
4. Action Archetype IV, Developing Inclusive Leadership Skills
5. Action Archetype V, Women World Wide
6. Action Archetype VI, Expatriate-Oriented Inclusive Leadership Development.

STRATEGY TO ACTION

Stressing Values in Practices

Our values demonstrate themselves in behaviors, as we have previously pointed out. Our biases, of course, are attitudes that may be prompted by our values. To the extent people can understand the impact of values and their worth, organizations can educate their employees toward inclusive attitudes and behaviors. As we know, the U.S. history is unique with its immigration-based roots that gave rise to values of social equality and upward mobility. Some U.S. experiences that include race relations produced legal and moral mandates that are at the root of U.S. diversity programs. However, North America with its largest percentage of foreign-born populations and the fewest number of official languages needs to include more ethnically relevant programs into diversity and inclusion trainings. The example provided in the What section addressed the most common value conflict area, that of individualism versus collectivism, relevant both for domestic/ pre-global and global organizations. Let us now see how this and other value-related issues can be intertwined into a broader context of U.S.-culture training programs, whether they "belong" to diversity or learning and development departments.

Action Archetype I, America the Diverse™

Transformational Diversity Strategy fit (here and in other Action Archetypes the first fit is always linked to the primary topic):
- Stressing values in practices
- Stressing differences of relevance
- Promoting organizational development of intercultural sensitivity

Goals
- Cross-group collaboration and workplace team-building
- Emotional intelligence to help you influence as leaders do
- Intercultural savvy to boost performance, capitalizing on U.S. diversity

Recommended Participants
- HR and diversity management
- Leaders responsible for bridging differences and values in conflict
- Members of diverse teams
- Participants of virtual and global teams

Core Content
- U.S.-American mindset – a big picture (stressing United States values that drive behaviors)
- National cultural values
- Main ethnic cultures of the U.S. and their impact
- Regional cultures of North America and their impact

Core Methodologies
- Contrastive-comparative analysis of presented data (promoting systematic understanding and ensuring retention of new knowledge)
- Statistically researched data consistently provided
- Experiential, action-based learning

Formats
- Lunch-and-Learn
- Half-day session
- Full-day classroom sessions

E-learning Options: Not applicable for this Action Archetype

Program Versions Available
- Understanding U.S.-American Cultural DNA and Becoming an Inclusive Leader
- Communicating with U.S.-Americans
- America The Diverse
- Communicating with Colleagues and Clients Who Speak ESL

Broader Context

The story of "America the Diverse" is that it was created on request, after one of our client company experts (coming from the corporate headquarters in North Carolina to New York) delivered his presentation in what was perceived as a southern style: leisurely, with an accent, and this style frustrated the important prospective customer so much that the nearly ready contract was jeopardized. Senior HR professionals then understood that they needed a program that would "teach all technical experts how to communicate in different regions of the United States, to attract — not turn away — the new customers." Consequently, leaning on a comprehensive book by Joel Garreau "The Nine Nations of North America" which describes how U.S. regional economics, mindset, and communication styles have been shaped over time, we developed a program that showed what distinguishes regional U.S. communities from the U.S.-American core culture, business-wise and social-wise.[2] The feedback from delivering this program suggested that even more specific in-depth knowledge was needed about mainstream U.S.-American culture and its subcultures. This knowledge was badly needed by recent immigrants and expatriates to the United States so that they could "figure out" their U.S. counterparts and fit in with national and corporate culture sooner rather than later. The new, content-rich program became increasingly popular with many diverse audiences and eventually grew into an equally popular "Communicating with U.S.-Americans." The outline below illustrates how the basic program is structured, stressing diverse U.S.-American values and differences of consequence and showing the U.S. workplace as an interdependent world and a whole entity. We then describe major ethnicities and the overtones they add to the national culture and conclude with ten regional U.S. cultures that also help shape certain values and communication differences.

Action Archetype I: Sample Outline
Understanding American Cultural DNA and Becoming an Inclusive Leader™

Description

Understanding American Cultural DNA is a critical program for growing inclusive leaders, who ensure productivity, performance and general business success through an in-depth understanding, right motivation, and inclusive communication style that appeal to employees of your organization. This is why it is important to see a big picture of increasingly diverse U.S. workforce. This workshop illuminates the true cultural identity of the United States, which can be described in terms of American Cultural DNA. From a national, internal U.S. perspective it is vital to increase awareness of the common values pertinent to the American culture while introducing a clear understanding of cultural, ethical, stylistic, and communication challenges of different cultural/ethnic groups and different regions in the United States. The program is designed to improve communication skills in a working environment that appreciates various modes of operation, both nationally and internationally.

Competencies Addressed
- Cross-group collaboration and workplace team-building
- Effective communication skills for inclusive leaders
- Emotional intelligence helping you influence as leaders do
- Intercultural savvy to boost performance capitalizing on U.S. diversity.

Diversity and Inclusion Issues Addressed
- Raising awareness of U.S.-American values, communication, leadership, and decision-making style for doing business in the U.S. successfully
- Understanding how stereotypes influence our perceptions of people from other cultures/areas
- Developing competencies to lead an inclusive, culturally diverse organization and become a true leader in a global marketplace
- Strengthening managers' ability to motivate and inspire diverse employee base using the best communication practices
- Leveraging intercultural diversity for business success, creating loyalty, identity, and the feeling of "one company" when people are spread over different locations.

Program Design

Pre-Training Work: Cultural Values Survey

Module 1. American Cultural DNA and Perceptions of U.S.-Americans: Starting on the Right Foot Can Go a Long Way
- DNA and Cultural DNA: the basics
- Understanding American cultural DNA
- Perceptions of U.S.-Americans

Module 2. America the Diverse: Seeing a Bigger Picture
- Breadth of territory and cultures
- American cultural DNA roots and variations
- Diverse mentalities and ethnic cultures
- U.S.-American national cultural values
- Regional cultures of North America
- Do you speak American?

Module 3. The Background Information You Need to Know
- High and low context cultures
- Styles of verbal communication
- Thinking patterns and characteristics evident in business communication
- Culture behind the scenes
- U.S.-American decision-making and communication
- Leadership U.S.-style
- Language as tool of management in the United States
- Key business interactions
- Audience expectations and listening habits

Module 4. Rules of the Game: Know Before You Go
- Communicating with U.S.-Americans: tips and techniques
- Business meeting protocol
- Socializing and small talk
- Business entertaining
- Etiquette and relationship-building
- Business women in the United States
- Case studies: What Went Wrong?

Summary and Takeaways (moderated discussion: Me team moving toward a perfect union; My personal action steps)

Lessons Learned for U.S.-Americans
- Diversity of workforce beyond awareness
- How to effectively interact with, manage, and market to diverse population groups
- What to keep in mind while working with diverse teams

Lessons Learned for Non-U.S.-Americans
- How to communicate and work with U.S.-Americans
- What to keep in mind when working in virtual teams or negotiating with or marketing to diverse population groups

Program Benefits
- Inspiring human capital to leverage new intercultural knowledge to enhance competitive advantage
- Understanding how stereotypes and unconscious biases are developed and showing managers how to embrace and support the many differences among employees
- Realizing that in the global business environment you need to integrate the perspectives of the representative cultures in the definition of problems, processes and solutions
- Putting to work the U.S. workforce agreement between the employee and the employer

as a multi-faceted give-and-take where growing mutual understanding, respect, inclusive leadership and diverse team-building are critical for business success.

Delivery Options
Understanding American Cultural DNA is available in three delivery options:
- Delivery by authors of the program. The length can range from 2-hour to half-day to 2-day, to special executive and board retreat sessions.
- Delivery by internal company trainers with licensing the complete program kit on CD-ROM—this maximizes program's per-person fee allowing to cover scores of managers with effective classroom training that creates behavior change. Train-the-Trainer sessions can be provided on an as-needed basis.
- Licensing the complete program kit for putting it on the company's Intranet. It makes web-based individual learning-on-demand accessible for all employees 24/7.

To help the new and not-so-new immigrants integrate should always be on the radar of diversity and all HR professionals, and to do so properly we need to educate them with respect to diverse U.S.-American cultures. Indeed, it is critical to introduce immigrants to mainstream national beliefs, one of which was recently polled by Gallup:

> Americans widely agree that the United States has a unique character because of its history and Constitution that sets it apart from other nations as the greatest in the world. This view, commonly referred to as "U.S. exceptionalism," is shared by at least 73% of Americans in all party groups, including 91% of Republicans.[3]

A possible interpretation of these survey results is that beliefs about U.S. exceptionalism may, in general, reflect a tendency to be patriotic when asked about the United States — which exacerbates the necessity of broadening the immigrants' and overseas subsidiaries' awareness of U.S.-American culture and of leveraging this knowledge for managerial and organizational effectiveness.

While underlining the basic structure of U.S.-American culture in Action Archetype I, we recommend the key points for new U.S. residents to understand and for potential immigrants to keep in mind. In this way, the program may be useful for domestic/pre-global diversity and also serve as a transition to global diversity developments. The pre-work for the program is based on questionnaires, either in electronic format or self-assessment online format.

Organizational Development of Intercultural Sensitivity

Organizational Development of Intercultural Sensitivity as a Transformational Diversity strategy model (described in Chapter 4) is the key for the Transformational Diversity framework. This strategy can be put into action using several different Action Archetypes, depending on current organizational priorities. However, Archetype II, Communicating Across Cultures, is the most versatile and most customizable because of its utterly flexible modules that allow for expanding one module while shrinking or eliminating another, based on organizational needs as perceived by human resources or as revealed by questionnaires and customization discussions with managers on the participants' side. As a result, the value discovery during the session can be enhanced by a number of activities ranging from "Contrasting values" to "Cultural values," to "Generational values," to "Team values," to "Values in conflict," to "U.S.-American values," and more.[4] This Action Archetype has such a wide applicability spectrum because it is about our core U.S.-American values compared and contrasted with those of people from different cultural backgrounds or countries. We live our values every day and may not be aware of certain problems rooted in our cultural composition (not personal attitudes) because cultural values change not only from country to country but also from organization to organization, and from one ethnic group to another. Let us take a closer look at communicating cross-culturally.

Action Archetype II, Communicating Across Cultures

Transformational Diversity Strategy Fit
- Organizational development of intercultural sensitivity
- Stressing values in practices
- Stressing differences of relevance

Goals
- To increase communication effectiveness for groups working in a diverse business environment
- To enhance synergy in international, diverse, multiple locations and teams
- To improve productivity and performance of all individuals working as a part of a culturally diverse team, both locally and globally

Recommended Participants
- Leaders responsible for bridging differences and values in conflict
- Members of diverse teams
- Participants of virtual and global teams

Core Content
- Culture and Perceptions
- Comparisons of High- and Low-Context Cultures
- How Different Culture Clusters of the World Operate
- Verbal and Non-Verbal Communication
- Redundancia: Foreign Language Simulation and Debrief
- Takeaways

Core Methodologies
- Contrastive-comparative analysis (ensuring systematic understanding and retention of new knowledge)
- Statistically researched data consistently provided
- Experiential, action-based learning

Formats
- Lunch-and-Learn
- Half-day session
- Full-day classroom sessions
- Train-the-Trainer option

E-learning Options Available
- Web-based application
- Electronic pocketbook (PowerPoint presentation with coordinated manual)

Program Versions Available
- Communicating Across Cultures
- No-Borders Communication with Clients
- Communicating with ... (country- or region-specific)
- The Diversity Experience: Rules of the Game (country- or region-specific)
- Communicating with People Who Speak ESL
- Communicating Across Invisible Borders

Broader Context

The program series can be used — first and foremost — for stressing values in practices (and beyond) to serve the purpose of epitomizing the major U.S. value to which Transformational Diversity clearly contributes: *e pluribus unum*, or unity in diversity, one that helps build inclusion, productivity, and performance and that is so crucial for all pre-global and global organizations. This Action Archetype II has the broadest reach as it stresses values in practices for employees who work domestically and communicate on a daily basis "across invisible borders" of different value sets, as well as for employees who work internationally and all speak the same language but face invisible borders of different values and perceptions that hamper their communication.

Focusing on Differences of Relevance

As noted above, differences of relevance are many in number, and each organization must determine the priorities to be addressed. These priorities typically include race, gender, age, and sexual or intellectual orientations, with priorities of ethnicities increasingly on the rise. A true respect for differences, perceived as respect by the people who need to be shown respect, is not innate and requires work (training and effort of understanding) on the part of those who need to show respect and inclusive attitudes. The broader understanding of cultural influences should become natural for all employees. The Transformational Diversity approach fits right in as it calls for understanding, recognizing, and rewarding both individual and group performances and the relationships between the two. We do not have to choose between individual and group performance but instead make sure that the relationship between them becomes meaningful in the workplace.

One of several tools to address differences of relevance is diversity coaching, which helps change behaviors and guide managers toward inclusiveness. Coaching helps by reorienting the mind when managers are trained in intercultural business competencies so that they can influence — and lead! — other people while using their personal, social, and structural motivations and abilities. Using somewhat different wording than we do ("coaching for inclusive leadership"), the "Influencer" group of authors gets to the core of the idea showing how remarkable leaders can be coached.[5] In our view, influencing is a trainable skill that can be developed in a series of group workshops or by individual, consistent diversity coaching. Diversity coaching is a powerful tool because it teaches the leaders-to-be to build and use time-released influencing as opposed to quick fixes.

Let us now turn to some specific differences of relevance — generational and regional differences — to see how to address leaders with the help of coaching. Coaching is not the only answer to tackle regional or generational differences; basic work can be done with group classroom programs and then continued with interpersonal face-to-face or telephonic sessions. In some very diverse settings, we can see that behaviors, values, and communication styles of good leaders have one invariant, one common denominator: inclusiveness that is expressed differently under the circumstances. As Deborrah Himsel suggests, we can extract this invariant and creatively apply it for coaching and feedback (like in the "give it to my face" situations in her book).[6] Inclusive attitudes of a leader cannot be missed; they are valuable, and these leadership tools and techniques are necessary. Here is a diversity coaching set up, as follows:

Action Archetype III, Diversity Coaching

Transformational Diversity Strategy Fit
- Stressing values in practices
- Stressing differences of relevance
- Organizational development of intercultural sensitivity
- Aligning domestic/pre-global diversity to global

Goals
- Global leadership
- Intercultural synergy in diversity
- Transition/developmental
- Remedial

Recommended Participants
- The new-to-management team leader
- The newly senior executive of diverse organization
- The manager/executive intent on enhancing his or her diverse team's performance
- The new-to-global business executive or manager: multicultural empowerment and leadership

Core Content
Step I, Initial Assessment(s)
Step II, Developmental Plans
Step III, Coaching process
Step IV, Action Training (blended learning relating to specific coaching areas)
Step V, Feedback to Manager/Human Resources

Core Methodology
- Utilizing two to four different assessments for inclusive leadership capability
- Using eight to twelve coaching sessions to gradually address issues and to develop an influencing style consistent with organizational practices and new needs

Formats
- Blended face-to-face and telephonic options available
- Individual/executive
- Group coaching

E-learning Modules Available
- Online assessments and evaluations
- E-mail inquiries and follow-up communication with a coach

Program Versions Available
- Diversity Executive Coaching
- Intercultural Diversity Coaching
- Group Coaching for Inclusive Leadership
- Global Inclusive Leadership Coaching

Action Archetype II: Sample Outline

Communicating Across Cultures

Description
Communicating Across Cultures is a foundational training program designed to provide a big picture of world culture clusters and lay down the basics of building workplace relationships for lasting business outcomes.

Competencies Addressed
- Communicating like inclusive leaders do
- Being culturally aware of groups working in a diverse/global business environment
- Effectively communicating with speakers of English as a second language
- Working productively as an integral part of a culturally diverse team, both locally and globally

Key Learning Points
- You will understand how culture impacts behavior, how perceptions affect one's ability to communicate across cultures, and how you may adjust your communication process and style for enhanced effectiveness at a diverse organization, locally in the United States and with international colleagues, partners, and multinational clients.
- By exploring different communication styles, perceptions, and thinking patterns, you will learn that what may be an effective communication for one group, organization, or

culture is not effective for another. This knowledge leads to understanding what steps need to be taken to enhance the effectiveness of intercultural communication.

- You will see that we can examine our personal, corporate, and national values through group activities, experiential learning, simulations, and debriefing. Together we will then establish how this examination affects our behavior in a diverse workplace, where we are likely to face our greatest challenges, and what tools can be used to leverage them.

Program Design Modules
- Cultural Dynamics: What is Culture?; Models of Culture; Cultural Flexibility; Culture and Perceptions.
- Redundancia: Foreign Language Simulation and Debrief. Takeaways: tools for efficient communication with people who speak English as a second language.
- High- and Low-Context Cultures: understanding the basics of communication divide and its relevancy for truly effective communication, employee motivation, and high performance in the workplace.
- Verbal and Nonverbal Communication: Everything we do and say communicates meaning that is interpreted through a cultural filter. You need to know the communication rules of the culture/people with which you are working in order to be successful.
- Communicating Across Cultures: Different communication styles and thought processes impact our interpersonal and intercultural business effectiveness. Learn how different regions of the world operate.
- Tools to use for enhancing communication with speakers of English as a second language:
  - › Clear and slow speech
  - › Small modules, repetition, summaries, and breaks
  - › Check up understanding indirectly (asking What-How-When questions)
  - › Pre- and post-meeting written message
  - › Yes does not always mean yes: what can we do about it
  - › Encouragement, relationship, and respect of values
  - › Understanding that U.S. reasoning style is different
  - › Detailed, clear specifics of the task assigned
  - › Visuals
- Implications for Doing Business and Conclusions

Action Archetype III: Sample Outline
Diversity Coaching

Description
Diversity Coaching is a one-to-one relationship with a coach tailored to the individual executive or manager or any high-potential individual. It involves coaching for impacting and motivating the diverse employee base, emphasizing the intercultural side of employee relations, to complement existing, typical coaching issues, such as coaching diverse men and women for career, for

global mindset, for competitive-cooperative behaviors; cautious risk-taking; relationship-building, and more. Diversity coaching aims at maximizing the professional effectiveness and growth in relation to inclusive leadership style, needs, and culture that affect the bottom-line results.

Competencies Addressed
- Gaining a more complete understanding of the strengths and development needs that coachees exhibit from the standpoint of their personal leadership competencies in a diverse workplace
- Improving global-scope decision-making, communication, and interpersonal competence, all of which — when addressed — yield better business results and return on investment

Assessments are used to appraise behavior and leadership capability on an as-needed basis over 8–12 coaching sessions:
1. 360-degree Leadership Assessment Tool (LAT)
2. Advanced Myers-Briggs Type Inventory (MBTI Step 2)
3. Others

Diversity and Inclusion Issues Addressed by These Coaching Types
- Global leadership
- Intercultural
- Transition/developmental
- Remedial

Coaching Process Design in Steps
- Initial assessment
- Developmental plans
- Coaching process
- Feedback to manager/human resources

Diversity Coaching Results
- Provide leaders with insights that enable them to manage more effectively cross-group and cross-culturally
- Focus on the key competencies and behaviors that enhance inclusive leadership behavior and capability
- Develop specific action steps that provide coachees with alternative methods to refine their behavior and to enrich their inclusive leadership skills

Broader Context

The coaching procedures may vary, and this Action Archetype presents ideas of how we can use Transformational Diversity coaching, be it for generational, regional, communication, cultural, or leadership issues. The example below may give you a broader context.

Example. A request from an HR director of a manufacturing company to an expert diversity coach was a mixed message: He could not reveal all the reasons why, but the company was having "problems with a certain young lady" (Marilyn). He said, "Please do whatever you can with her; train or coach her, but this is her last chance to improve, and she knows it." The man is about the kindest soul one could meet in the higher echelons of human resources, but he could not conceal his resentment of the coachee-to-be because, although an excellent professional, she "did not fit the company's culture" and had ongoing conflicts with her supervisor and peers, and she generally "put on airs." Soon the diversity coach started working with Marilyn, a New Yorker who was transferred from the New York office to South Carolina, where her "unfitting" began. Marilyn admitted she disliked the S.C. office culture from day one; its tempo, communication style, and hierarchical structure were "very much unlike me," she said. She made no friends there and requested to be transferred back to New York; in fact, many of her account clients were from New York State. This came to be a clear diversity training/coaching case. The expert coach led Marilyn to carefully assess her South Carolina colleagues and to understand the cultural, generational, and geographical differences that pervaded their actions and communication styles, and through this understanding came acceptance (inclusion). As a result, Marilyn learned how to better position and express herself in her new office, to be appreciated by the locals, and finally to "fit in." She was also coached on generational issues, on how to behave with her senior colleagues and managers (for most of the people in the S.C. office were older than she was), on how to show the respect the elder executives expected, and on what to do to contribute more on the job.

The point. Diversity coaching may be just the next "it" thing to do on our way to becoming mindful and respectful about differences of relevance. The diversity of U.S. culture is common knowledge, and it is not only about race-gender-ethnic minorities but also about regional and generational differences. Addressing these differences of relevance in a timely manner is necessary to retain high-potential staff and talent.

Specific Needs

When looking to identify the most important differences of relevance for your organization, you may want to look into the specific needs of the workforce, which, from a Transformational Diversity perspective, can be categorized as to the following:

- Leadership needs
- Talent development needs
- Organizational culture needs (including female leadership)
- Employee group needs

Let us discuss how Transformational Diversity can meet those needs.

Leadership and talent development needs may be best addressed with respect to differences of relevance as Transformational Diversity strategy, such as understanding links between individual behaviors and inclusive practices and motivating and leading multicultural human capital. All needs, including organizational culture and employee group needs, can be met in various ways:

- Holding a series of diversity roundtables, designed to continually monitor the leadership's new needs as they arise and to keep leadership abreast of the new Transformational Diversity initiative needs while discussing how to motivate a diverse workforce and mitigate intolerance

- Conducting a series of diversity experience seminars to counteract stereotyping and to promote multiculturalism using the "learn while doing" approach

- Implementing diversity coaching to instruct individuals and groups on inclusive behaviors and on motivating an increasingly diverse workforce across cultures. A series of programs like these certainly make business sense as they promote inclusion in the most tangible way, thus mitigating intolerance and stereotypes and preventing conflict. Many of the programs are covered by Action Archetype IV.

Action Archetype IV, Developing Inclusive Leadership Skills

Strategy Fit
- Stressing values in practices
- Stressing differences of relevance
- Aligning domestic/pre-global diversity to global diversity

Goals
- Promote cross-group and cross-functional collaboration and team-building
- Develop emotional intelligence to help you influence as leaders do
- Acquire competencies and skills to lead in an inclusive manner in a culturally diverse organization
- Strengthen managers' ability to implement the best practices of inclusive leadership for business success

Recommended Participants
- Team leaders and emerging leaders
- Newly senior executives of diverse organizations
- High potentials and new talented hires
- The new-to-global business executives or managers

Core Content
- Understanding Transformational Diversity and Inclusive Leadership
- How to Achieve Strategic Objectives
- Influencing Up and Down the Ladder
- Inclusive Leadership Skills: Principles and Techniques
- Activity: Planning and Practicing Inclusive Leadership Skills

Core Methodology
- Contrastive-comparative analysis of presented data (promoting systematic understanding and ensuring retention of new knowledge)
- Statistically researched data consistently provided
- Experiential, action-based learning

Formats
- Lunch-and-Learn
- Half-day session
- Full-day classroom session
- Train-the-Trainer option

E-learning Options Available
- Web-based version of some programs
- Electronic pocketbook of some programs (accompanying the Train-the-Trainer option)

Program Versions Available
- Leveraging Intercultural Know-How for Inclusive Leadership Skills
- Transformational Diversity Executive Roundtables for Raising ROI
- Leveraging Generations for Inclusive Leadership Skills
- Teambuilding and Influencing for Raising Productivity
- Individual Coaching/Training for Leadership
- Executive Dine-and-Learns: Menu for Inclusive Leadership

Action Archetype IV: Sample Outline
Leveraging Generations for Inclusive Leadership Skills

Description
This interactive workshop offers a unique perspective on generational issues. It is designed for enhancing synergy at a workplace, building a more integrated and effective organization. The emphasis is placed on identifying biases/stereotypes; on learning about generational cultures, perceptions, and expectations; and on gaining the knowledge of how to attain the full cooperation of other generations. Guidelines for recruiting, motivating, and retaining the new generation of employees are offered and discussed.

Leveraging Generations for Inclusive Leadership Skills can be customized for the particular workplace to support mutual understanding of employees in the inclusive business environment, thus promoting synergy and cooperation across the board.

Competencies Addressed
- Cross-group and cross-functional collaboration and team-building
- Emotional intelligence to help you influence and manage as leaders do
- Intergenerational mutual understanding to boost cooperation, productivity, and performance

Diversity and Inclusion Issues Addressed
- Raising awareness of different generational perspectives
- Understanding how stereotypes influence our perceptions of people from other generations and vice versa
- Acquiring competencies and skills to lead an inclusive, generation-wise diverse organization
- Strengthening managers' ability to implement the best practices in managing the generation gap and to leverage diversity for business success

Program Design

Module 1: Understanding Generations: Personal and Lifestyle Characteristics
- Generation timelines
- Personal and lifestyle profiles by generation
- Generation elasticity (activity)
- How diverse perceptions and emotional intelligence affect one's ability to communicate across generations (simulation)
- Understanding generations Q&A

Module 2: The Conflict Zone: Achieving Strategic Objectives
- Security versus stability
- Recognition the key
- Youthful ambition
- Independence and functional competence
- Communicating across generations (activity)
- Big picture and strategic objectives
- The Conflict Zone: Achieving Strategic Objectives Q&A

Module 3: Principles and Techniques of Leveraging Generations
- Us and Them: values to be respected
- Down and Up the Ladder (case studies and debrief)
- In the Middle
- The Baby Boomers and the Xers
- Principles and Techniques Q&A

Module 4: Unlocking the Mystery and Developing Inclusive Leadership Skills
- The Power of Four
- Engaging Every Employee for Retaining the Best Talent
- The Latest Wisdom on Retaining, Training and Tapping into Generation (X, Y . . .)
- Activity: Developing Generation-based Inclusive Leadership Skills
- Unlocking the Mystery Q&A

Summary: Q&A, Takeaways, Evaluations, and Wrap-up

Program Benefits
- Inspiring human capital and empowering them to leverage generation diversity and to achieve a competitive advantage
- Becoming aware of the generations' identity, perspectives, and cultural assumptions built into all communication exchanges and the pitfalls of those assumptions
- Learning to communicate effectively with Baby Boomers and Generations X and Y
- Getting the tools for developing Inclusive Leadership Skills

Broader Context

Example. A well-known research company with a little over 500 employees, mostly in the United States, sent a request for leadership coaching/training for one of the recently promoted directors. Requests like this rarely come from that company, and comments from the senior HR professionals sounded somewhat condescending, for example, "Our new VP, Pauline, said she needs individual leadership coaching because her team is very diverse, and she finds it difficult to influence and lead them in a culturally sensitive manner — but why did she seek the position in the first place? You call yourself a leader — you should be able to figure out your leadership issues on your own!" Diversity leadership coaching/training had been provided to Pauline, and after its completion at the end of three months both upper management and her diverse team gave complimentary reviews of this VP's performance and her inclusive leadership attitudes.

The point. We believe that both HR professionals and senior management, need to be trained to be aware that in our diverse workforce everyone deserves a fair chance to be a leader and that human resources' first line of duty is to present its people with maximum opportunities to grow on the job — because however evident this truth is for many, it may not be understood by others in the organization. Leadership coaching/training is especially important for developing the new leaders at diverse companies.

Organizational culture needs have many aspects, such as becoming an employer of choice based on fostering an inclusive workplace; making respect for diversity a corporate value; instituting communication changes; offering specific programs for women that address engagement and recruiting; reflecting inclusion and opportunity without unconscious bias; providing upward mobility for high potentials; and promoting leadership roles for women in a global company. These needs are met by program series such as Women's Strategic Career Planning in Competitive Fields, designed to facilitate interactive exercises teaching how women's diversity of mind — as different from men's — can help women increase collaborative-competitive styles, take smart risks, pursue goals with propriety and positive energy, and build effective business relationships.[7]

The multitude of Organizational Culture needs is covered by Archetypes I though VI, depending on current priorities. Let us now look at Archetype V.

Action Archetype V, Women World Wide

Strategy Fit
- Stressing differences of relevance
- Promoting organizational development of intercultural sensitivity
- Aligning domestic/pre-global diversity to global diversity

Goals
- Understanding gender diversity in terms of inherent capabilities, values, and decision-making processes
- Looking at cultural traits through women's lenses to help them foster a working environment that ensures successful intercultural and intergender communication
- Women learning how to survive and thrive in any culture —as a part of it, as expatriates, or working with people from this culture locally or virtually
- Learning how to be effective with bosses, colleagues, and clients alike, thereby building stronger relationships and strengthening their leadership across cultures
- Gaining new insights through experiential learning, simulation, quizzes, and debriefings

Recommended Participants
- High-potential and emerging female leaders
- Talented women of diverse organizations
- New female hires
- Men who manage women

Core Content
- Module I. Cultures, Perceptions, Global Mindsets
- Module II. Cultures and Women's Positioning: Comparing Apples to Apples
- Module III. Leveraging Women's Strengths for Leadership and Career
- Experiential Learning (Reincarnation activity)
- Structured Activity for Developing Inclusive Leadership Skills (Takeaways)

Core Methodology
- Contrastive-comparative analysis of presented data (promoting systematic understanding and ensuring retention of new knowledge)
- Statistically researched data consistently provided
- Experiential, action-based learning
- Case studies with analysis and debrief

Formats
- Lunch-and-Learn
- Half-day session
- Full-day classroom session
- Train-the-Trainer option

E-learning Options Available
- Electronic pocketbook of some programs (accompanying the Train-the-Trainer option)

Program Versions Available
- Women World Wide: Know-How for Leadership and Career
- Women Across Cultures: Counteracting Unconscious Biases
- Women World Wide: Global Perspective for a Global Mindset
- Leveraging Gender for Inclusive Leadership Skills
- Organizational Savvy for Women in Competitive Fields

Action Archetype V: Sample Outline
Women World Wide: Know-How for Leadership and Career™

Description
In our day and time organizations need to grow overall productivity while ultimately utilizing the input of women, who constitute up to 50 percent of today's workforce. This program focuses on different mentalities, culture patterns, and perceptions of women in different countries, exploring diverse cultural norms and their impact on women's positioning and subsequent participation in the workforce and societal affairs. Participants will be sensitized to different nation's "rules of the game" with respect to women, which help in maximizing collegial and client relationships, limiting the influence of stereotypes, and growing synergy, productivity, and teamwork.

As we discussed, women are naturally inclined to be inclusive leaders; all they need to be broadly recognized as such is to be aware of their own strengths, to learn how to use them to win more friends and followers, and to advance their careers while working with people of different cultural mindsets — transcending cultures and genders. Five activities during the session culminate in Leveraging Culture and Gender for Leadership Skills, a rehearsal of putting the knowledge acquired at this session to work.

Competencies Addressed
- Communicating effectively across cultures and genders
- Gaining in-depth understanding of how to address men-women workplace issues for career development

Diversity and Inclusion Issues Addressed
- Counteracting unconscious biases
- Understanding the positioning of women worldwide
- Acquiring knowledge of how to be an influencer in a diverse organization
- Strengthening women's ability to find the way to become inclusive leaders

Program Design in Three Modules (current focus on BRIC countries: Brazil, Russia, India, China; customization to select regions/countries is part of the program)

Introduction
- Your personal targets
- Agenda: what we do
- Our training methodology: how we do it

Module I. Women World Wide: Cultural Dynamics
- Women Influencers and Leaders: We've Got Talent (warming-up activity)
- Cultures and Subcultures: perceptions
- Big Cultural Divide: high and low context (information)

Module II. Cultures, Mentalities, and Women's Positioning: Comparing Apples to Apples
- Pragmatic Mentality and Culture Patterns
- Women in North America and Australia
- Holistic Mentality and Culture Patterns: Southeast Asia
- Women in China and other Southeast Asian Countries
- Strategic and Tactical Tips for Businesswomen
- Abstract Thinking Pattern, Mentality, and Culture Patterns
- Women in Brazil and Latin America
- Strategic and Tactical Tips for Businesswomen
- Abstract-Emotive Mentality and Culture Patterns
- Women in Russia: Positioning, Traditionalists, and the "New Rich"
- Strategic and Tactical Tips for Businesswomen and Businessmen
- Analytical Mentality and Culture Patterns: Northern Europe, North America, Australia, South Africa, and India
- Strategic and Tactical Tips for Businesswomen
- Reincarnation (Experiential Learning activity)

Module III. Leveraging Women's Strengths for Leadership and Career
- Gender Gap or Gender Stylistics? (information on strengths and discussion)
- Women versus Men: Stereotyping at the Workplace
- Redirecting Your Perfectionism
- Gender Differences in Leadership: Agree or Disagree?
- Men-Women Teamwork (prioritize two out of six benefits)
- Strategies for Upward Mobility: It's All in Style! (information)
- Eyes on the Prize: How to Leverage Your Strengths
- Quiz: U.S. Businesswomen (activity)
- Leveraging Culture and Gender for Leadership Skills (activity with a prompt: drawing a behavior-communication chart of the person you want to influence, and then laying down a basic road map to improve the relationship for influence, upward mobility, and leadership; discussion/debrief to follow)

Summary: Takeaways and Wrap-Up

Benefits
- Participants will understand cultural diversity in terms of values and decision-making processes.
- All participants will be able to look at cultural traits through women's lenses to help them foster a working environment that ensures successful intercultural and intergender communication.
- Female participants will learn how to survive and thrive in any culture — either they are a part of it, or they are expatriates, or they are simply working with people from this culture locally/virtually.
- Female participants will learn how to adapt their communication style to be effective with managers, colleagues, and clients alike, thereby building stronger relationships and strengthening their leadership across cultures — all while gaining new insights through experiential learning, simulation, a quiz, and debriefings.

Broader Context

An abundance of publications on gender issues is available, and one can also pick up some golden nuggets from related discussions on the Internet. We agree with many other authors that because of the historical stratification of communities, a kind of self-limitation of women (and some other groups) became institutionalized, and as a result women were educated to avoid conflicts with the ruling men — and they got used to seeking complementary roles. A series of specific trainings will challenge these self-imposed limitations on women's ambition and at the same time will slowly but surely erode conscious and unconscious biases with respect to women in the workplace at large — until it becomes unnecessary to take care of the numbers (i.e., desired percentages of women) imposed by upper management for compliance when hiring or promoting, as these numbers will take care of themselves. Most importantly, in our experience focusing on gender issues paves the route toward inclusion over all other dimensions. Working on female leadership issues and on gender awareness of all employees deserves to be central to the efforts of diversity professionals.

That said, let us admit that we have a problem with many excellent traditional publications on gender issues: they provide well-arranged facts using the inductive approach to organizing them, which hinders translating the data into practical training, the inclusive leadership development for women — which is one of our goals. For this reason, in designing Action Archetype V, we took a deductive approach for organizing the training sessions. We have drawn upon the core neurological research of men-women differences, which expose the strengths and weaknesses of women as they are related to workplace productivity and upward mobility. Historically, outstanding women of all times could turn their weaknesses into strengths — and prevail — so we searched for techniques to teach women en masse, or every woman, how to make friends and become inclusive leaders, that is, to effectively use the skills they have a predisposition to. This major innovation became Action Archetype V.

Another innovation is more of a "developing awareness": Module II of this Action Archetype explores how women are faring within five different cultural clusters, on average, and points out some tips as to how businesswomen from other cultures are perceived and expected to behave in various cultural environments.

As we discussed in early, the retention and development of women in the workforce is a critical business imperative. With this focus, we see corresponding developments in work/life practices such as expanded customization of jobs to accommodate those who want to work part time or take extended leaves — all with the intent of retaining valuable talent. In this regard, both men and women are the beneficiaries.

Aligning Domestic Diversity to Global Diversity

Many diversity professionals of global companies agree that aligning domestic diversity to global diversity is a tough assignment with too many unknowns and no acceptable blueprint available. For a number of reasons, as discussed previously, Transformational Diversity places this alignment at the forefront, making it one of its four core strategies.

Employee group needs are the focus of this alignment. For example, for the new hires on-boarding the introduction of the organization as an inclusive entity should be key. In addition, intercultural training for recent immigrant populations should receive special attention, and intercultural awareness training and communication training for the broad employee population should be the focus for raising productivity and performance. This task can be accomplished in different ways and then used to foster intercultural understanding of diverse employee groups, thus preventing conflict and avoiding stereotyping, both locally and globally.

Since Transformational Diversity is all about inclusion and inclusive leadership behaviors, the above-mentioned strategy implementation can be supported by Archetypes I through VI — based on organizational priorities at the time. Probably the clearest way to begin is to embrace the populations concerned with working on a global arena: expatriates and long-term travelers, as well as employees engaged in virtual teams. Archetype VI as presented below offers the perspectives and needs of these specific employee groups.

Action Archetype VI, Expatriate-Oriented Inclusive Leadership Skills

Strategy Fit
- Aligning domestic diversity to global diversity
- Stressing differences of relevance
- Promoting organizational development of intercultural sensitivity

Goals
- Learn to use "cultural lens" to fully understand the new business environment, to develop necessary emotional intelligence, and to build useful relationships
- Acquire intercultural business competencies and skills to lead in an inclusive manner in a culturally diverse organization

- Strengthen expatriates' ability to implement the best practices of inclusive leadership for business success

Recommended Participants
- Expatriates-to-be pool of managers
- Emerging leaders working in multicultural or virtual teams
- New-to-global-leadership executives of diverse global organizations

Core Content
- Cultural dynamics: a framework for global mindset and skills development
- Comparing cultures and communication styles
- Comparing leadership styles across cultures
- Culturally appropriate inclusive leadership traits (leadership styles, decision-making, delegating, coaching, giving feedback, conducting meetings, resolving conflicts, and more)
- Ethics and etiquette as building blocks for relationship-building
- Skill-building: individual and group activities

Core Methodology
- Comparative analysis of presented data (promoting systematic understanding and ensuring retention of new knowledge)
- Statistically researched data consistently provided
- Experiential, action-based learning
- Case studies with analysis and debrief

Formats
- Lunch-and-Learn
- Half-day session
- Full-day classroom session
- Train-the-Trainer option
- Ongoing coaching

E-learning Options Available
- Electronic Library for Global Mobility and Leadership (series of CD-ROM-based pocketbooks consisting of a PowerPoint presentation and coordinated manual, country-specific)

Program Versions Available
- Managing Across Cultures (series)
- Communicating with (country X): Intercultural Power Briefing
- Leveraging Intercultural Business Competencies for Global Leadership
- Business Passport to (country X)
- Team Building for Expatriates and Locals: Blending Cultures — Building Strengths
- Expatriate Express (Lunch-and-Learn series)

Action Archetype VI: Sample Program
Managing Across Cultures for Global Leaders (day one)

60 minutes	**Culture and Perceptions** • What is culture? • What is cultural awareness? • Perceptions: a simulation

Learning Objective: We establish what cultural baggage we bring with us when working with people from cultures different from our own. By examining our own management styles we are able to determine what is effective in which parts of the world.

75 minutes	**The Communication Process** • Stereotypes of U.S.-Americans around the world • Verbal and nonverbal behaviors • Differing communication styles and other cross-cultural barriers that can inhibit effective communication in social and business settings • Verbal and nonverbal communication • High and low context • Communicating across cultures: effective techniques

Learning Objective: By examining the differences between direct and indirect communication, we establish what is effective when communicating with people from other cultures, either in face-to-face situations or by telephone, e-mail, or fax. Participants gain practical tools for real intercultural communication situations.

60 minutes	**Business Ethics, Etiquette, and Protocol** • Complexities of protocol • Gift-giving and entertaining • Dress code • Anatomy of a typical business meeting • Showing appreciation

Learning Objective: The objective is to examine our national business ethics, etiquette, and protocol and verify what messages we communicate to others. We examine how our business behaviors affect international relationships and determine how successful long-term intercultural relationships can be formed.

60 minutes	**Lunch**

90 minutes	**Managing Across Cultures** • Identification of values that typically constitute U.S.-American's cultural profile contrasted with those of the other value systems in general. We discuss: • How our values are reflected in our own business behavior • How our behaviors may be misperceived by business people overseas • Strategies for minimizing and averting potential misunderstandings in the culturally diverse workplace • Core values critical to understanding the mindset of people from the target culture mindset

Learning Objective: The objective is to present and discuss core intercultural business principles, both national and corporate, as they may be relevant to the current company business practices. The ACROSS framework (Appendix 2) is used to examine the target cultures and to develop strategies.

75 minutes	**Business and the Workplace (joined by Host National)** Presentation and discussion with Host National on cross-cultural business values and how approaches may differ in areas such as leadership, teamwork, decision-making, adherence to hierarchy, importance of relationships, conflict resolution, work ethic, social etiquette, lines of communication, and corporate environment.

45 minutes	**Case Studies and Business Application** • Case studies: four to choose from • Analysis and discussion of case studies depicting cross-cultural misunderstandings occurring between U.S.-Americans and other nations in typical social and business settings

Learning Objective: By exploring culturally determined leadership and decision-making styles and clashes that occur during negotiations, we can examine ways to respond in a more productive and positive way, thereby influencing the success of the outcome. An action plan for effective leadership, decision-making, and negotiation will be developed.

30 minutes	**Intercultural Adaptability: Becoming an Inclusive Leader** • A look at self: strengths and weaknesses • Where I can improve?: personal action plan of leading and managing across cultures • Debriefing and program evaluations

Managing Across Cultures (day two, country-specific: for example China)

3 hours	**Learning Styles and Effective Communication** (Chinese Business Communication Expert) • The cultures of China • Written communication • Information exchange • Communication and perceptions

Learning Objective: The way we process information is a direct result of our systems of education. We examine how the Chinese view learning and how the value of those learning styles affects the process of communication. Participants will compare and contrast the Chinese communication style with their own and identify areas of challenge and commonality.

1 hour	Lunch
3 hours	**Conducting Business with the Chinese** • Business protocol • Leadership style • Delegating, coaching, and giving feedback • Meetings/Presentations • Sales/Marketing • Negotiations • Decision-making • Relationship-building • Customer service • Recruiting

Learning Objective: Participants will gain a valuable perspective on doing business successfully with the Chinese. Participants' specific needs are determined before the training, and topics are adjusted accordingly.

1 hour	**Values Clarification** • Comparing and Contrasting Cultures • Traditional versus Nontraditional Values in the U.S. and China • ACROSS framework to examine the Chinese culture and to develop strategies (see Appendix 2 for details)

Learning Objective: Values clarification is essential for proper intercultural understanding. A facilitator will examine the cultural values of China and how they compare to the business value systems in the participants' own cultures. The participants develop an awareness of where the greatest potential for trouble may lie and how they might avoid those pitfalls. Participants are given the chance to prioritize their own cultural values and to assess the importance of certain values for their Chinese counterparts or clients.		
0.5 hour	Debriefing and Evaluation	

At the National Foreign Trade Council conferences in July 2010 and 2011, attendees discussed the industry tendency for mobility and the necessity of providing leadership development for expats and employees who work with overseas offices on a regular basis. This is new for mobility, a welcome change. If we look to the roots of this change, we can see why it has occurred:

- Traditional transactional cross-cultural training for expatriate families is limited and does not provide the necessary skills on the job.

- The need to compete globally pushes companies to focus on necessary competencies, such as expat-oriented leadership development and skill-building, and this need is growing.

Although many companies realize that in the new economy expat-oriented leadership development is a requirement to survive and thrive, implementation is stagnant because of the following reasons:

- A clear concept of what to do is absent.

- A clear understanding of how to do it is absent.

- Big commercial and mobility vendors are ill-equipped to design and customize the group-based expat-oriented leadership skills development — only a qualified professional education service can do the job.

Thus, global companies have good intentions, but all too often their heterogeneous thinking and lack of a clear concept or plan fails to produce the desired outcomes. In a broader context of expatriate-oriented leadership development, what are the prospects? This is a question well worth discussing.

First, although the practice of preparing expatriates for overseas assignments through cross-cultural training has developed into mainstream orthodoxy in the business, academic, and government communities, the return on investment of training strategies is open to debate, writes Ray S. Leki.[8] Here we cannot agree more because across-the-board satisfaction with the efficacy of training efforts remains incomplete. While Leki describes some important facts of the neurophysiology of the brain that explain some of the gaps between intercultural training intentions and real performance, we would like to bring up another pitfall, or rather, intercultural minefield. This minefield is about the inherent insufficiency of traditional expatriate and spouse cross-cultural training, which overlooks the whole host of necessary intercultural business competencies that can make the assignment succeed or fail. Professional educators have long known that intercultural business competencies — or skills — can be effectively trained only in a group setting of peers, where expats-to-be or global leaders-to-be experience the effect of appropriate training methodologies at work. This approach is very different from a training session in the comfortable company of your spouse who is thinking about important family issues in the first place. Therefore, the mobility-based cross-cultural training typically called "Living and Working in …" is geared mostly to "living," while the coverage of "working" only scratches the surface.

Second, if the organizations can afford to provide two-day training for the expatriate family — fine! However, if within the same budget they want a better ROI on preparing expatriates, they need to reallocate funding, knowing that a group business competencies training for future global leaders should become a must. Yet another must is expatriate coaching for leadership.

Third, the relationship between international assignments and leadership skill development has been well documented in sources offering some answers, most of which are beyond our scope.[9] But as we have advocated throughout this book, we share a commitment to the integration of intercultural skills acquired by expatriates into the entire organization. This integration can only begin to happen through a commitment of adequate resources and qualified training expertise.

PRACTICAL REMARKS ON TRANSITIONING FROM DOMESTIC/PRE-GLOBAL TO GLOBAL DIVERSITY

We have mentioned these two issues throughout the book: the ever-expanding cultural diversity of the U.S. workforce and the need for all organizations to be globally prepared by aligning their "domestic" programs with global diversity. However, this alignment is easier said than done. Some organizations have already made considerable strides in this direction, and benchmarking is possible. Yet, organizationally speaking, many companies still remain ethnocentric in both their diversity-leadership developments and in their expatriate appointments, and they have not yet progressed in establishing globally integrated strategies and processes for preparing their populations as future global citizens and global leaders.

The challenge for domestic (or pre-global) leaders — and especially for diversity leaders — is to prepare for the organization's global expansion and to be able to develop employees' competencies in a way that is appropriate for the global leaders in diversity. We will share with our audience how this alignment can be attained and which programs can help jump-start the process. First, we suggest using U.S.-American business competencies from a cultural framework.

Interculturalists know well that to be able to fully understand other people and their cultural makeup, we need to gain a good understanding of our own culture — where we are coming from and what our own cultural values are — and then, only then, will we be able to effectively connect with others and to treat them in a culturally sensitive manner. While every (national) culture is unique in its own way and can be examined for its generalized norms, the specifics of the U.S.-American cultural framework seem to be prevalent not only in the U.S. workplace but also in some of the global areas it touches. For this reason, understanding of U.S. culture should be a departure point for U.S.-Americans connecting with the world at large.

Earlier, we pointed out some basic U.S.-American values that are in conflict. Let us now think about another value, a sense of optimism, as an example: optimism is said to be endemic in U.S.-American culture

— as different from so many others. This endemic, culture-embedded optimism and associated risk-taking lead to what is known as "group think": after 9/11 many people thought that chasing Osama bin Laden in Afghanistan could be the right thing to do and that the risk would somehow take care of itself. A similar thing happens every day in business, when U.S.-Americans, typically goal-oriented and generally prone to risk, get frustrated because their partners with different national backgrounds and typically risk-averse, take too long making decisions, "dragging their feet," and demanding heaps of additional information before starting on any new initiative.

Certainly, overall U.S. business has made big strides in the global markets despite culture differences regarding optimism and risk-taking vs. more safeguarding, risk-averse, cautious approaches. However, the success of U.S. businesses has not been optimal. Why not is a big question, and the reason is basically cultural. For instance, the norm for U.S. managers is to be frank, explicit communicators; direct, self-reliant, rugged individualists; and short-term planners quick to act — these are perceived as all-positive characteristics of our management here in the United States. But in an international context, behavior like this may bring about some big misunderstandings, relationship-destroying confusions, or even conflicts, because in many other cultures the norm is different: indirect, implicit communicators oriented toward group interests and long-term planners who are very cautious to proceed — these features are characteristic of good management overseas. Unfortunately, our U.S. managers seldom have the opportunity to be trained in international business culture before they plunge into global business; and learning on the go has no safety net, which is necessary in a global arena, and is saturated with many risks.

The global business world requires us to be increasingly culture-wise. In the United States, many people are inclined to under-appreciate the impact of culture on business, much more so than people do in other countries. We tend to think that if we treat people the way we ourselves want to be treated, then everything will be fine. Not so. In fact, in interacting with people from other cultures (and countries), we need to treat our counterparts the way *they want or expect* to be treated, according to their cultural norms. We must acquire the ability to stand in their shoes; we need to be able to understand their moral imperatives while seeing the world through their eyes — only then will we know what their decisions are likely to be. When all our managers are culturally sensitive enough to act like this, we will become globally prepared and optimally successful in a globalized economy.

With this concept in mind, we can begin connecting values while implementing "America The Diverse" Action Archetype I (as described above), starting with understanding the basic, mainstream U.S.-American values and the diverse values of our minority populations. After we fully understand the makeup of our U.S.-values, we can progress to understanding how other cultures see us, based on our own culture-conditioned perspectives of the world. In other words, first focusing on U.S.-American culture is a pragmatic way to commence Transformational Diversity learning because it can be used to transition to an in-depth understanding of other cultures in the world. We advise this approach to transitioning from domestic/pre-global to a truly global corporate culture and to the global diversity that preconditions it.

In our experience, paralleling training in the United States with international location application is a good idea, and the team-building programs work well for promoting inclusion and teamwork, resulting in high performance. Most organizations had their fair share of failed global efforts because of the differences of relevance — as they struggled with the effects of becoming increasingly more global — and they should know better than to repeat costly mistakes. Bringing together the two teams — as we did once when separately training the U.S.-American and Singaporean teams on intercultural business competencies — across continents, and thus clearing the major differences of relevance, made the project a success while enabling the U.S.-American team to be better globally prepared for productive teamwork with their counterparts overseas, and vice versa. We need to remember, though, that any department, business unit, or temporary grouping of people for a specific project constitutes a team, and local, domestic teamwork is as important as global. These training sessions always convey important lessons, the most important being that pre-global and global trainings should be interconnected. From cross-cultural based teamwork, adjusting this lesson to a multicultural team environment is possible — whether at home or across an ocean.

How to Team-Build Across Cultures

Using the *Six Dimensions of Cultural Diversity* for intercultural team-building is possible, as is exploring the particular dilemma of value dimensions and how they can be reconciled.[10] However, we probably cannot include all of these dimensions in a single, one-day training that has a defined timeframe. Therefore, it proved fruitful to customize the sessions based on what the participants — and human resources — deemed critical issues at that time. The two-day mirrored team-building sessions can be accomplished using Action Archetypes IV and VI, as presented above.

Communicating in respectful terms with international counterparts or clients, or with colleagues in the cubicle next to yours, involves understanding diversity. Thus, diversity directors and consultants need to focus not only on determining commonalities — like they do in affinity groups — but also on anticipating personal divergences that lead to conflicts and difficulties, or in other words to cultural dissonances. The training for achieving a balance in a team goes beyond race and gender, shifting the focus from traditional issues to minorities-integration-synergy-performance issues. This focus needs special attention as minorities and overseas employees and clients may present a complex host of issues, including cultural backgrounds and thinking styles.

Let us now consider some other examples of how organizations are becoming globally prepared. A practical example of linking pre-global U.S. diversity (and managing with intercultural sensitivity in the United States) to global diversity issues is a "Managing Across Cultures" program as a sample realization of Action Archetype VI. This program (above) starts with identifying possible cultural baggage that global employees may bring with them when working with counterparts from cultures different from their own. The program, allows participants to compare stereotypes of U.S.-Americans around the world to some stereotypes that we, U.S.-Americans, hold about some other cultures — and a clear vision helps us to use this knowledge productively. Step-by-step, we contrast perceptions, values, business behaviors, and communication patterns of our own versus targeted culture(s) and then see how the global diversity unfolds. Intercultural adaptability is certainly trainable. The experiential learning activities and case studies effectively help us demonstrate the process to achieve optimal retention of new knowledge. We also provide consistent comparisons of cultures and communication styles, making use of comparative and visual methodologies, including R. D. Lewis' diagrammatic form, to expose how different nationals expect to communicate with and influence interlocutors, audiences, colleagues, and business partners.[11] Participants of the "Managing Across Cultures" program come out of the training with an enriched global mindset and clear ideas of how to deal with global diversity and managing business for ultimate success.

Example. A huge chemical company grew its multinational subsidiaries and general global presence, partly through acquisitions. The cross-cultural communication issues also grew, exponentially. Finally, a procurement director decided to train her metropolitan New York staff on "how to" do business right with their overseas counterparts. While customizing the program with management, she identified 10 diverse cultures that were the "most difficult to deal with." Facilitators had been tasked before with delivering one-day sessions to the employees who needed intercultural grooming on a number of cultures, but never before had they needed to cover ten cultures in one day. An appropriate, multiple-issue program customization (see Appendix 2), coupled with the creativity of Eric J. Kruger, the facilitator and author of ACROSS, brought the program on target.[12] The group enjoyed the training so much (joking, laughing, and sharing their own cases to be resolved) that in the evaluations the participants unanimously asked "Why only one day? We want more!" How did Eric cover ten cultures in one day, a huge challenge to any trainer? This expert facilitator lost no time, asking at the start a critical question: "Is there a culture that — for you — is really the biggest stumbling block?" And all twenty-two participants responded: China! Then, beginning with and allowing more time for China, Eric led the group through Chinese values that drive behaviors, and while discussing the communication tools for dealing with colleagues in China, he pointed out (whenever appropriate) the tools that may also be applicable for Hong Kong, Singapore, Japan, Taiwan, or sometimes even India. Thus, he combined a country-specific briefing with the bigger picture, and presenting a bigger picture while consistently comparing and contrasting issues with the U.S.-American standpoint strengthened retention of the newly acquired knowledge and effected broader skills application. The manual, specially designed for this session, was recommended for posttraining enhancement and for reading more details about specific countries.

The point. Diversity leaders need to integrate this kind of training for global business mindset into all their learning programs targeting global diversity. A program like this makes business sense and achieves practical results, as upper management will soon notice and will in response increase its support of the initiative.

Creativity and Transformational Diversity

By cultural default, U.S.-Americans and the ways they conduct business differ from business professionals and practices in many other nations; this fact and other related issues have historically not been adequately addressed. However, a new generation of diversity HR professionals is emerging, and these open-minded, creative individuals are willing to go in new directions and are eager to address diversity/inclusion development in new ways.

Some diversity directors of the new generation are showing genuine interest in Transformational Diversity, in particular in (a) global preparedness and developing intercultural business competencies, (b) entertaining new ideas and innovative training approaches, and (c) foundational intercultural training. These practitioners connect the new skills and the new possibilities of diversity today.

In working toward global preparedness, creativity pays. The progression of Action Archetypes I through VI, coupled with inspiring evaluations from participants, makes Transformational Diversity popular within the company fairly quickly. Employees learn inclusive behaviors and discard stereotyping in a natural way, without mulling over words like "diversity" and "inclusion"; they genuinely like acquiring the new skills the Transformational Diversity way. This shows that Transformational Diversity is furthering the human capital's diversity of mind and promoting inclusive behaviors and intercultural business competencies, nationally or internationally. Simply put, we believe that entertaining novel ideas (like educational lunch-and-learns, intercultural training, and experiential learning) to develop competencies for global diversity preparedness is what distinguishes the new generation of diversity directors.

Lastly, we would like to exemplify Action Archetypes I and II, America the Diverse and Communicating Across Cultures. Specifically we would like to explain how they can be creatively used for building on domestic diversity to suit both pre-global and global diversity needs.

All programs under Archetype I work well for domestic diversity in all U.S. companies: U.S. Census data from 2007 show that 19.7 percent of people nationwide speak languages other than English at home and that this number is snowballing with growing immigration.[13] More specifically, speech is certainly a useful corporate success tool used by different nationals in many different ways, and Action Archetype Program III lets one learn how to effectively communicate with diverse people who speak English as a second language — to prevent conflict and to avoid stereotyping while contributing to synergy, productivity, and overall performance. Hence, human resources and diversity managers need to pay closer attention to communication because integrating a diverse workforce takes time and effort. Action Archetype I is a first step toward including employees in a manner that is respectful, while motivating them at the same time. From upper managers to line managers to rank-and-file employees working in diverse teams, the participants of this program will understand how language is intertwined with culture and how to recognize the greatest intercultural-interlinguistic challenges and how to make use of the tools that leverage them. They will also learn how to adjust their communication and management styles for enhanced effectiveness with both local and distant coworkers as well as with multinational clients.

We recommend Action Archetype II, Communicating Across Cultures, as the second step in transitioning from domestic to global diversity. The logistics are clear: Action Archetype II provides a progressively larger picture of cultural diversity worldwide. All sessions covered by this Archetype are packed with simulations, exercises, and information covering verbal and nonverbal communication, high- and low-context culture styles, and more — they are customized to the participants' needs. Even the foundational Lunch-and-Learn sessions, lasting 90 to 120 minutes, incorporate techniques to tackle stereotyping and to ensure practical inclusion skills learning. For these reasons, all Action Archetype II sessions can be effectively used for domestic/pre-global diversity trainings as well as for transitioning to global diversity trainings; succinct and short, the trainings help the people who want to be inclusive but often do not know how.

While some companies do have a physical global presence, the workforce in their U.S. offices often feels some disconnect with other countries and cultures. They are unsure how to behave in a culturally sensitive manner with occasional expats or with visiting colleagues from overseas, and they feel frustrated in certain situations, even when exchanging sometimes confusing e-mails with counterparts from other countries. What is the proper way to handle such situations in a culturally appropriate manner? In brief, Action Archetypes I and II are the answer and a quick fix for starters; they highlight strategies and basic communication "how to" tools. They brief diverse audiences on U.S. culture and on global culture clusters and show how to bridge typical communication gaps strategically and tactically. A good transition from pre-global to global diversity training, the sample programs are offered in the outline form above.

Using Internet-Based Applications

All six Action Archetypes described above go hand in hand with Internet-based applications that complement instructor-led sessions or that are used as standalones in many cases. Let us now discuss why and how online and CD-ROM-based learning can contribute to Transformational Diversity outcomes by creating an inclusive leadership culture and intercultural business competencies that ultimately enhance an organization's bottom line. In previous chapters we maintained that Transformational Diversity is a vision that is redefining traditional diversity programming with the help of inclusion, and inclusive behaviors can and should be trained. Should the training be traditional instructor-led or technology-based (that is, using CD-ROMs or the Internet)? Which method is most appropriate for Transformational Diversity implementation? Learning professionals have discussed the advantages and disadvantages of these kinds of trainings for quite some time now. Since the effects of Transformational Diversity on organizational culture and the bottom line are presumed to be both positive and tangible, the importance of media for implementing it cannot be overstated. So we will review some of the benefits and drawbacks of different media approaches, keeping in mind three implementation principles: first, we need our inclusion training to influence the hearts and minds of participants; second, we need the new knowledge and inclusion skills to be retained and put to work; last, we need to train on an ongoing basis and on a progressively massive scale.

Let us take a closer look at how different learning media compare, summarize them, and then see which can be used most effectively for Transformational Diversity initiatives implementation.

- Classroom training advantages: interactive human contact; ultimate customization for specific groups; accommodating of different learning styles; best retention

- Classroom training drawbacks: presumed higher costs

- CD-ROM-based training advantages: affordable; unlimited license cost; self-paced learning; allows easy access to content for a global workforce; has an instructional design that creates entire modules/lessons

- CD-ROM-based training drawbacks: lack of human-instructor interaction; distribution of physical materials with updated content requires redistribution (unless access to the CD-ROM is also provided via company intranet); does not accommodate personal learning styles

- Web-based training advantages: affordable per-employee cost; self-paced learning; easy access to content for a global workforce; content is easily updated on the server-computer

- Web-based training drawbacks: lack of human-instructor interaction; does not accommodate personal learning styles; lack of multimedia (only text and graphics)[14]

Reflecting on a Choice of Media

Reports determining the return on investment for e-learning across different studies show that employees' time spent on training is reduced by about 40 percent using both kinds of e-learning, CD-ROM and Internet, which means that people learn faster. This metric, cited when comparing classroom to e-learning, is understandable. What comes as a surprise is the conclusions that retention and transfer of new knowledge with electronic media also improve — although this advantage is concurrently claimed by both in-classroom and e-learning advocates, so more research is needed here. As far as costs are concerned, the figures indicate that e-learning saves approximately 20 percent in the first year of implementation, while in the second and third years when development costs are not the factor, the savings rise to nearly 50 percent.[15]

Bram Groen and Alexandra Parrs provide a useful summary of the key academic observations about virtual learning and its distinction from distance learning.[16] Their research concluded that intercultural communication education, which applies to Transformational Diversity education, should become a regular component of any intercultural skills development, from introductory to advanced levels.

Above, we pointed out three principles to keep in mind for adequate Transformational Diversity initiatives implementation (influencing hearts and minds, retaining knowledge and putting inclusion to work, and rolling out initiatives on a progressively massive scale). Which media will work best, taking into account advantages versus drawbacks? The answer is *specific blended learning*, which means an initial reliance on traditional classroom training and increasingly complementing it with Internet- and CD-ROM-based learning. We advise launching Transformational Diversity initiative implementation with instructor-led training for the following reasons:

- Content customization to organizational culture matters in Transformational Diversity initiatives more than in other subject areas because it is more defined by specific company demographics.

- Influencing minds face-to-face has a greater persuasive power and will "recruit" more followers of inclusive behaviors than will word of mouth or computer-based content.

- Putting Transformational Diversity/inclusion to work is better activated through live group interaction and human contact with the instructor.

As we can see, the first two principles can be satisfied with classroom training. However, to satisfy the third principle (rolling out Transformational Diversity initiative on an increasingly massive scale), which is critical for the anticipated practical Transformational Diversity outcome, we definitely need to make more use of e-learning. Let us recommend some e-learning applications that proved to work well and are in harmony with the Transformational Diversity approach.

For a general background on diversity and inclusion learning, an online course, "Global Diversity and Multicultural Competence,"[17] is a good idea. It has a self-assessment component and covers the meaning of diversity, culture, and inclusion; the business case for diversity; and the connection to leadership and values. It can be supplemented by more specific classroom courses, for example, courses for women's career planning.[18]

For specific Transformational Diversity-oriented learning for inclusive behaviors, we recommend a "Library for Global Diversity," which comes in CD-ROM format and includes Electronic Pocketbooks covering different topics; these pocketbooks can be used as CD stand-alones or online, when installed on organization's intranet. This is a systematic, sustainable source of learning about cultures, exposing all kinds of stereotyping and broadening the horizons of a global mind-set. The Library can be used as a standalone tool or complemented by classroom training. This application typically involves the licensing of Electronic Pocketbooks and creating a Library for Global Diversity step-by-step. Each pocketbook is a coordinated two-piece set: a manual with a coordinated PowerPoint presentation.

Tools of this kind have been designed for people doing business internationally or working as part of a diverse team. They focus strictly on business communication issues and on fostering politically correct intercultural sensitivities and business communication skills and know-how. Electronic libraries and other similar tools allow organizations to extend programs to all employees:

- All users will learn how to do business in a culturally appropriate way, be it with colleagues overseas, in their own country, or with clients all over the world.

- Expatriates will acquire the absolute must-have knowledge of their new country.

- Corporate trainers may use the professional script (as part of a manual) and a coordinated PowerPoint presentation to reinforce their own training of employees on an as-needed basis and as many times as necessary.

For promoting inclusive behaviors and avoiding conflict situations on both business and social levels, an online condensed intercultural reference guide can serve perfectly. Many such tools are available, and they are often accompanied by online questionnaires of various levels of sophistication; they all deserve attention. A number of tools called "Intercultural Knowledge Base" can be customized and installed on a company's intranet. The basic themes covered on each country include the most important topics for inclusive business communication:

- Communication styles
- Business etiquette
- Management style
- Meeting and greeting
- Making appointments
- Business dress code
- Welcome versus unwelcome topics of conversation
- Addressing colleagues with respect
- Nonverbal communication
- Appropriate business gifts
- Business entertaining
- Business meetings
- Teamwork
- Women in business
- Negotiating

Tools of this nature provide practical, basic tips for culturally correct business communication and behavior; they also alert users to intercultural sensitivity as a basis for establishing relationships and enhancing business. The fees for tools like this range from tens of thousands of dollars per year (based on user count) to free of charge (in a package with other services.) HR leaders' research and knowledge of the vendor market will lead them to select the appropriate tool for their organization.

FUNDING TRANSFORMATIONAL DIVERSITY

For diversity professionals willing to move ahead with Transformational Diversity, funding the new ideas and developments is a natural question. With no attempt to provide any recipes, we would like to summarize the relevant funding suggestions coming from discussions with some HR professionals:

- First, the "old" diversity budgets can be tightened to a certain extent. Diversity "old style" became much less affordable as many of its actionable pieces became cost-prohibitive in an atmosphere of general thriftiness. These pieces included costly off-sites, luxurious accommodations for regional diversity conferences and routine affinity group gatherings, and investing in cost-prohibitive online self-profiling questionnaires that did not help develop global diversity. The funding should be redirected to the plenty of practical diversity programs available.

- Second, internal collaboration of diversity and training departments allows them to split their training budgets for Transformational Diversity purposes, creating a win-win situation for both departments when they both get credit for contributing to a healthy organizational culture. Available funding needs to be shared and redirected to intercultural business competencies trainings that provide more tangible contributions to potential economic restoration.

- Third, internal trainers and staff can do some Transformational Diversity training instead of outsourcing it to consultants. This practical solution is made possible by licensing certain programs from consulting organizations that provide packages of content, presentations, handouts, and such — which allows the company to save time on designing the programs and on replicating delivery on an as-needed basis.

- Last, since upper management largely controls final funds allocation, its buy-in into Transformational Diversity ideas and outcomes will help support a consistent effort toward an inclusive leadership culture of the company as a whole. In our experience, waiting until the organization's leaders realize that "old" diversity is outdated will be too late, and HR directors will be left stumbling to retain the workforce. An effective way to involve upper management is to hold regular briefings or discussions during which the diversity staff members, along with their consultants, introduce the need(s) for the Transformational Diversity initiative, including the facts and figures substantiating proposed solutions, and then prompt the business managers for their opinion. Regularity of open discussions is the key.

TRANSFORMATIONAL DIVERSITY BENEFITS

Our Transformational Diversity vision represents our efforts to promote incorporating intercultural competencies into domestic, pre-global, and global organizations primarily in the U.S. and North American environments. This process connects the dots between established domestic diversity programming and global diversity, for which all organizations need to be prepared. The business case for diversity remains defined based on beliefs in the value of conflict for the better good — for innovation, creativity, and well being. Scholars continue to struggle with and uncover the sources of bias, ethnocentrism, and racism that will help them enlighten us over time in some new ways. We note as a positive development, in particular, the work at Harvard University by Todd Pittinsky and others on "allophilia" — the liking for other groups — that would seem to counter the negative attitudes attached to diversity.[19] For the time being, we rest our case with education and training as the hope for the new diversity breakthroughs.

In sum, implementation of our vision of Transformational Diversity can offer a number of benefits to diversity practitioners. Among them, we count the following:

- Enhanced teamwork, productivity, and performance, which boost an organization's competitiveness and bottom line
- The ability to engage all levels of employees
- A focus on inclusion as action to help us strengthen organizational cultures and be respectful of all diversity variables by geography and organizational relationships

- Learning and learning reinforcement strategy aligned with the organization's mission, vision, goals, and performance systems

- Actionable efforts to prepare organizations globally, which is integral to global diversity

- New skills and competencies to enhance inclusive leadership and a total culture of inclusion, resulting in higher loyalty of our human capital

Chapter 6. Thinking and Acting Anew — Now!

Transformational Diversity is a new vision of diversity developments that revises and transforms traditional diversity programming flow through an infusion of an intercultural perspective acquired by intercultural business competencies training and programming. It offers new possibilities not only for global but also for pre-global (domestic with international interests) North American companies by helping their organizational cultures work efficiently and by cultivating their global preparedness. Transformational Diversity focuses, first and foremost, on inclusive practices and cultures that contribute to a productive, engaging, and just workplace that will enable companies to survive and thrive. These practices create tangible effects on the bottom line — making Transformational Diversity a miracle worker amid tough economic times, as opposed to typical stagnating "domestic" diversity programs that are unable to help improve companies' financial situations or adequately meet their employees' needs.

Employees tire of mandatory diversity sessions that provide barebone prescriptions only, with no real medicine to follow. There is no medicine for the tired "old" diversity; the only medicine that works is the shift of focus from the old, traditional diversity routine to inclusion-oriented intercultural business competencies training. This practical approach demonstrates to employees the real skills needed to perform better, to be better appreciated, and to feel better on the job. While the world economy is recovering from global financial disaster, diversity will return to normal too, but it will be a new normal for diversity, just as for the economy as a whole. The financial crisis has left many scars and a heavy legacy of debt on balance sheets of many organizations — which is why Transformational Diversity, designed to contribute heavily to the bottom line, has a bright future helping companies stage their comeback.

The notion of Transformational Diversity as a new diversity norm has already convinced many diversity leaders, even if some do not agree with every aspect of its approach. Transformational Diversity is obviously a new wave in diversity developments, and as such it has received criticism from practitioners who, for various reasons, adhere to the old diversity programming. Nonetheless, the stormy present of the current economy calls for innovative thinking and action, and Transformational Diversity happens to be an effective instrument that allows corporate human resources to inspire, motivate, and rise to the occasion as true leaders do.

As we have tried to show in this book, Transformational Diversity is based on principles of rationality, common sense, and pragmatism — not on any time-honored set of traditional practices. It is based on employees' and companies' need for boosting a return on investment — not on emotions and a comfortable allegiance to old diversity programming. Shifting to a Transformational Diversity focus from a traditional race-gender focus is bold, but not too bold. Diversity managers need to negotiate with upper management as to how to redirect current diversity efforts and to endow them with a new meaning, instead of routinely continuing to ask for more funding for a convenient, well-beaten path. Transformational Diversity today is the *off-the-beaten path*, an innovative trend. It is a trend well matched to these tough economic times, and diversity managers, with the approval of upper management, need to either implement it today or be left behind because they failed to empower their human capital in the spirit of the time.

From a perspective of addressing the burning issues in a timely manner, it may be appropriate to remember what Rev. Martin Luther King Jr. called "the fierce urgency of now" back in 1963. This sense of urgency is very fitting in today's situation of furthering diversity development: now is the time to make real the action of Transformational Diversity and inclusive leadership — and to motivate our human capital to give 100 percent of their productivity. We cannot pass on this reliable resource of boosting the return on investment (ROI). After companies largely exhausted the resource of layoffs, we as a nation and corporate U.S.-America in particular, need to preserve the integrity, loyalty, and effectiveness of our remaining workforce. In our day and time, shrinking from this responsibility is not an option.

The onset of Transformational Diversity requires fundamental changes in regular diversity practices — and, **first of all**, changes in the attitudes and behaviors of the upper management of organizations. The leaders need to abandon their previous understanding of what diversity is (or used to be) and become open to new ideas, adopting a modern concept of Transformational Diversity that fits our current economic conditions and helps us improve productivity, performance, and ROI in the unheard-of proportions. We believe that organizations should start thinking holistically with respect to this area and its meaning for their workforce. Certainly, moral support, involvement of the upper management, and personal examples of inclusive leadership are crucial for success.

Second, implementing Transformational Diversity — making use of a customizable road map provided in this book — requires a visionary and almost dogged approach and effort on the part of those in charge of the initiative.

Finally, and most importantly, management needs to remember that only appropriate and timely *funding* will yield tangible results sooner rather than later. This process may not be easy, but the payoffs are considerable.

So to make a leap to Transformational Diversity we need to focus not on the easy way out but on the greater good: "What is best for my company is best for me, and I'll go for it." For organizations, it is time either to shine with Transformational Diversity or to drift into oblivion. The choice is clear.

Appendix A. Milton Bennett's Development Model for Intercultural Sensitivity (DMIS)[1]

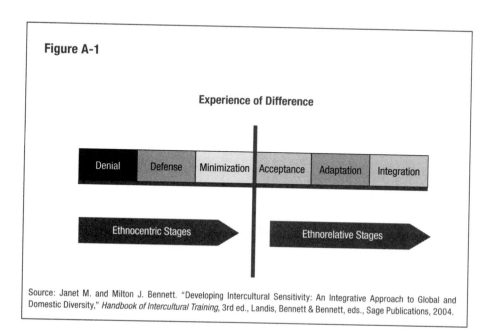

Figure A-1

Experience of Difference

| Denial | Defense | Minimization | Acceptance | Adaptation | Integration |

Ethnocentric Stages

Ethnorelative Stages

Source: Janet M. and Milton J. Bennett. "Developing Intercultural Sensitivity: An Integrative Approach to Global and Domestic Diversity," *Handbook of Intercultural Training*, 3rd ed., Landis, Bennett & Bennett, eds., Sage Publications, 2004.

Ethnocentric stages: ethnocentricism is broadly defined as those unconscious stages whereby people experience their own culture or values as the focus of reality.

1. *Denial of difference:* Milton Bennett claims that the denial stage is the purest form of ethnocentrism, in that individuals simply choose not to consider cultural differences. In organizational terms, this denial amounts to being ignorant about cultural issues or having no diversity training beyond the basics required for legal compliance reasons.

   › Identifiers: Avoidance of the subject of cultural diversity; references to "them"; monocultural management; probably no systematic efforts on behalf of cultural diversity in recruitment and advancement processes.

2. *Defense:* The defensive stage of ethnocentrism perceives some specific cultural differences to be threatening. In organizational terms, discrimination against other cultures may appear. Power is demonstrated through defending particular positions against others and feeling a pressure to assimilate.

   › Identifiers: Corporate overconfidence; showing cultural difference is to be avoided; internal perceptions of "us versus them"; pressure for newer or minority groups to assimilate, causing some reverse discrimination, or even "backlash" actions.

3. *Minimization:* Minimization is the final stage of ethnocentrism whereby differences are recognized but made minimal through a mindset that claims "we are all alike," and by focusing on cultural similarities.

   › Identifiers: Belief that technology is advancing cultural convergences; active support for universals; global practices and policies that acknowledge "one size does not fit all" but a limited ability to adjust for differences.

Ethnorelative stages: In Bennett's terms, the broad contrast of ethnorelativism to enthocentrism comprises first acceptance and then ultimately integration of differences into one blended culture. While this picture may be aspirational, it is based on the assumption that cultures and related cultural behaviors are best understood as relative to one another, or within contexts. It, too, is composed of three stages:

1. *Acceptance:* Differences and cultures are accepted and respected within the organization.

    › Identifiers: Active efforts to recruit a diverse workforce; internal review of policies and practices to accommodate differences; beginnings of local adaptation to global policies; some "talk" aspects but few efforts or skills to manage differences.

2. *Adaptation:* With increasing cultural contact adaptation occurs. Adaptation is characterized by demonstrated new skills and behaviors, which Bennett stresses as additive and not necessarily substitutive features. Adaptation is a process. For individuals, adaptation may be evident in the ability to shift one's cultural frame of reference, as in communications. For organizations, adaptation is characterized by active commitments to training in matters of intercultural competence.

    › Identifiers: The process of review includes taking different perspectives into account, expanded training in inclusive mindset, developing a skill set of intercultural competence, and considering differences as resources for teamwork and organizational effectiveness.

3. *Integration:* Integration as a final stage is complex, but it essentially allows for individuals to come to grips with their cultural identities so that they can see themselves existing within any number of them in healthy ways. Individuals dealing with integration issues, as Bennett reminds us, are generally bicultural or multicultural in their worldviews.[2] In similar fashion, organizations demonstrate integration by an ability to examine every aspect of their activi-

ties in their cultural contexts and then by making appropriate accommodations.

> › Identifiers: Institutionalized commitment to examining all policies and actions in their cultural context; little emphasis on national identity of the organization, if a global company; effective use of diversity and inclusion throughout the organization's practices and reward systems.

Appendix B. The ACROSS©
Cultural Business Model*

The ACROSS© Cultural Business Model is a multifaceted model useful for analyzing and comparing business values and management styles in different cultures. It is easy to use, can be Internet-based and used in online training, and permits immediate comparison by visual scanning. At the heart of the ACROSS© Model is a set of cultural variables directly relevant to today's global and multicultural business environment. The variables are arranged in six major themes:

A = Attitudes, Beliefs, and Cultural Values

C = Communication and Information-Sharing

R = Relationships, Trust, Gender, and Hierarchy

O = Operations: Decision-Making, Time, Risk, Change, and Resources

S = Sales, Persuasion, Negotiation, Pricing, and Money

S = Style of Management, Motivation, and Teambuilding

The ACROSS© Model is intentionally designed to be easy to remember. Hence its name, a mnemonic derived from the initial letters of the six major themes.

Each of the six themes of the ACROSS© Model contains six pairs of cultural variables, or dimensions. Thus, the Model contains 36 cultural dimensions and 72 variables. Examples of such cultural dimensions are "Information-sharing versus Information-withholding" and "Holds that time is short" versus "Feels that time is abundant."

ORIGINS AND DEVELOPMENT

The ACROSS© Model has been developed by Eric J. Kruger, a cross-cultural specialist with extensive international experience in the global business and government arena. He has selected the Model's 72 cultural variables from the following:

1. An exhaustive review of the cross-cultural literature, including the original practitioners, such as Geert Hofstede and more recent innovators such as David C. Thomas

2. An experience in current international business

3. Eric J. Kruger's own research and practice from twelve years of intercultural work

The model has been rigorously tested in over 2,000 real-life training and executive coaching sessions and reviewed by a multinational panel of cross-cultural specialists. It receives ongoing updating every three months, given today's rapidly changing and unpredictable environment. It is thus fully up-to-date, incorporating such issues and practices as global financial reregulation, virtual team-building, and outsourcing.

THE DISTINCTIVENESS OF THE ACROSS© MODEL

The ACROSS© Model has a number of exclusive features that enhance its usefulness, applicability, and comprehensiveness:

- Its unique feature is that it permits a directly visible identification and comparison of much more than the national business/management Unlike most of the cross-cultural models reviewed, which are often developed in an academic environment or from a sociological or anthropological perspective, the ACROSS© Model focuses

---

* *EXPERT MS Inc.* has exclusive world rights to the ACROSS© Model.

specifically on *management and the world of work*, whether this be business, government, the health sector, or other areas.

- The Model addresses much more than national culture. It includes such critical facets as corporate or organizational culture and gender/age culture. Again, to permit easy assimilation and memorization, the facets are grouped into six sets:

  SPACE: Nation, region, city

  SECTOR: Industry/sector, organization, department

  FUNCTION: Profession/educational training, rank, role

  ATTRIBUTE: Age, gender, civil status/background

  INDIVIDUAL: Personality, management style, work style

  TIME: Business cycle, political setting, social mood T

- Finally, the Model explicitly addresses money and pricing. To the authors' knowledge and surprise, it appears to be the only cross-cultural model to do so.

APPLYING THE ACROSS© MODEL

The ACROSS© Model is easy to use and can be applied with a modicum of explanation in a business meeting, training course, or executive coaching session. The Leader, Facilitator, or Coach explains the essence of the ACROSS© Model, its purpose, content, and methodology to the participants, clarifies a few of the less familiar variables, and invites the participants to review the dimensions relevant to their work thoughtfully and carefully. They then score themselves on the dimensions. Subsequently, the scores of the countries, cities, industries, or professions of direct interest to the participants are provided, drawn from the extensive database upon which the Model is based.

In figure B-1, the participant (marked by an X), is a U.S.-American senior-level chemical engineer from Michigan. She works in a major health products corporation (marked by CO) located in northern New Jersey. She is being relocated to Mannheim, Germany, to work in a joint venture for two years. The scores below reveal that U.S. managers in the health industry are relatively individualistic in the workplace (though not as individualistic as, say, day traders in the financial industry, who score a 1). The company in question (COM) is somewhat more group-oriented than U.S. companies in this industry (USH). Ms. X, coming as she does from the U.S. industrial Midwest, is more group-oriented, but not as group-oriented as her new German counterparts. The implications of this situation can then be addressed.

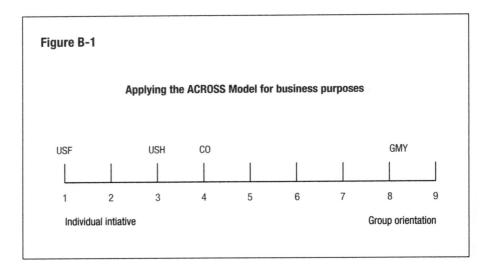

Figure B-1

Applying the ACROSS Model for business purposes

USF   USH   CO   GMY

1   2   3   4   5   6   7   8   9

Individual intiative   Group orientation

Bibliography

Abdallah-Pretceille, Martine. "Interculturalism as a Paradigm for Thinking about Diversity." *Intercultural Education* 17, no. 5 (2006) 475-483.

Adler, Nancy J. *International Dimensions of Organizational Behavior.* 4th ed. Florence, KY: South-Western Press, 2002.

Babcock, Pamela. "Survey: Many Leadership Development Programs Too Tactical." Society for Human Resource Management. May 22, 2008. www.shrm.org/Publications/HRNews/Pages/DevelopmentProgramsTooTactical.aspx.

Bartz, Carol, "Leadership in the Information Age," *The Economist: The World in 2010*, special edition, November 13, 2009, 128.

Bennett, Janet M., and Milton J. Bennett. "Developing Intercultural Sensitivity: An Integrative Approach to Global and Domestic Diversity." In *Handbook of Intercultural Training.* 3rd ed. Edited by Daniel Landis, Janet M. Bennett, and Milton J. Bennett, 147-165. Thousand Oaks, CA: Sage, 2004.

Bennett, Milton J. "Towards Ethnorelativism: A Developmental Model of Intercultural Sensitivity." In *Education for an Intercultural Experience*. Edited by R. Michael Paige, 21-71. Yarmouth, ME: Intercultural Press, 1993.

———"A Developmental Model of Intercultural Sensitivity." Available at www.library.wisc.edu/edvrc/docs/public/pdfs/SEEDReadings/intCulSens.pdf.

Black, J. Steward, Hal B. Gregersen, Mark E. Mendenhall, and Linda Stroh. *Globalizing People through International Assignments*. Reading, MA: Addison-Wesley, 1999.

Boggs, Dave. "E-Learning Benefits and ROI Comparison of E-Learning vs. Traditional Training." SyberWorks. 2009. http://www.syberworks.com/articles/e-learningROI.htm.

Briscoe, Dennis R., Randall S. Schuler, and Lisbeth Claus. *International Human Resources Management: Policies and Practices for Multinational Enterprises*. 3rd ed. New York: Routledge, 2008.

Cohen, Alan. BrainyQuote. http://www.brainyquote.com/quotes/quotes/a/alancohen188584.html.

Connerley, Mary L., and Paul B. Pedersen. *Leadership in a Diverse and Multicultural Environment: Developing Awareness, Knowledge, and Skills*. Thousand Oaks, CA: Sage, 2005.

Cumulative Gallup Workplace Studies. Available at www.gallup.com.

Frankel, Barbara. "What Does Management Reveal about Global Diversity Management?" DiversityInc. July 8, 2010. http://www.diversityinc.com/article/7851/What-Does-Research-Reveal-About-Global-Diversity-Management.

Friedman, Thomas L. *The Lexus and the Olive Tree: Understanding Globalization*. New York: Anchor Books, 2002.

———*The World Is Flat: A Brief History of the Twenty-First Century*. Farrar, Straus and Giroux. New York, 2005.

Gallup, "Americans See U.S. as Exceptional; 37% Doubt Obama Does" (December 22, 2010). Available at www.gallup.com/poll/145358/americans-exceptional-doubt-obama.aspx.

Gardenswartz, Lee, and Anita Rowe. *Diverse Teams at Work: Capitalizing on the Power of Diversity*. Alexandria, VA: Society for Human Resource Management, 2002.

Garreau, Joel. *The Nine Nations of North America*. Boston: Houghton Mifflin, 1981.

Global Diversity and Inclusion: Perceptions, Practices and Attitudes. A Study for the Society for Human Resource Management (SHRM) conducted by the Economist Intelligence Unit. Alexandria, VA: Society for Human Resource Management, 2009.

Groen, Bram, and Alexandra Parrs. "Bringing Cross-Cultural Communication Education into the 21st Century — Virtually." *Intercultural Management Quarterly* 11, no. 3 (Fall 2010): 3-7.

Grove, Cornelius N., and Willa Zakin Hollowell. "Globalizing Diversity: The Two Dilemmas Facing Global Corporations." 2008. http://www.grovewell.com/pub-global-diversity.pdf.

Hall, Edward T., and Mildred R. Hall. *Understanding Cultural Differences: Germans, French and Americans*. Yarmouth, ME: Intercultural Press, 1990.

Hampden-Turner, Charles M., and Fons Trompenaars. *Building Cross-Cultural Competence: How to Create Wealth from Conflicting Values*. New Haven, CN: Yale University Press, 2000.

Himsel, Deborrah. *Leadership Sopranos Style: How to Become an Effective Boss*. Chicago: Dearborn Trade, 2004.

Hofstede, Geert. *Cultures and Organizations: Software of the Mind: Intercultural Cooperation and its Importance for Survival*. New York: McGraw-Hill, 1997.

Hofstede, Geert, Gert Jan Hofstede and Michael Minkov. *Cultures and Organizations: Software of the Mind: Intercultural Cooperation and Its Importance for Survival*. 3rd ed. New York: McGraw Hill, 2010.

Hollander, Edwin P. *Inclusive Leadership: The Essential Leader-Follower*. New York: Psychology Press / Taylor & Frances, 2008.

Hubbard, Edward E. *How to Calculate Diversity Return on Investment*. Petaluma, CA: Global Insights, 1999.

Huffington, Arianna, "The Year of Hope 2.0," *The Economist: The World in 2011*, special edition, November 22, 2010, 42.

Hymowitz, Carol. The New Diversity. In: "Leadership — The Journal Report," *Wall Street Journal*, November 14, 2005.

IBM. "Diversity 3.0™." Available at www-03.ibm.com/employment/us/diverse.

Johansson, Frans. *The Medici Effect: Breakthrough Insights at the Intersection of Ideas, Concepts, and Cultures*. Boston: Harvard Business School Press, 2004.

Kluckhohn, Florence Rockwood, and Fred L. Strodbeck. *Variations in Value Orientations*. Evanston, IL: Row/Peterson, 1961.

Kruse, Kevin, and Jason Keil. *Technology-Based Training: The Art and Science of Design, Development, and Delivery*. San Francisco: Jossey-Bass, 2000.

"Definition of Intercultural Competence." Kwintessential. Available at www.kwintessential.co.uk/articles/info/definition-intercultural-competence.html.

Lackey, Susan. "Expert: International Diversity Programs Need Backing from Top." Society for Human Resource Management. Available at www.shrm.org/hrdisciplines/global/Articles/Pages/DiversityProgramsNeedBacking.aspx.

Landis, Dan, Janet M. Bennett, and Milton J. Bennett, eds. *Handbook of Intercultural Training*. 3rd ed. Thousand Oaks, CA: Sage, 2004.

Laroche, Lionel, and Dan Rocherford. *Recruiting, Retaining and Promoting Culturally Different Employees*. Oxford: Butterworth-Heinemann, 2007.

Leki, Ray S. "Reality Therapy for Intercultural Training." *Intercultural Management Quarterly* 11, no. 3 (Fall 2010): 12.

Lewis, Richard D. *The Cultural Imperative: Global Trends in the 21st Century*. Boston: Intercultural Press, 2003.

———. *Cross-Cultural Communication: A Visual Approach*. 2nd ed. Winchester, UK: Transcreen Publications, 2008.

Lieberman, Simma, George F. Simons, and Kate Berardo. *Putting*

Diversity to Work: How to Successfully Lead a Diverse Workforce. Mississauga, ON: Crisp Publications, 2003.

Mayer, Kathryn C. *Collaborative Competition™: A Woman's Guide to Succeeding by Competing.* Collaborative Competition Press, 2009.

McKinsey & Company. *The War for Talent: Operation and Leadership Practice.* April 2001.

Mor Barak, Michalle E. *Managing Diversity: Toward a Globally Inclusive Workplace.* Thousand Oaks, CA: Sage, 2005.

Miller, Frederick A., and Judith H. Katz. *The Inclusion Breakthrough: Unleashing the Real Power of Diversity.* San Francisco: Kaleel Jamison Consulting Group, 2002.

Noer, David M. *Healing the Wounds: Overcoming the Trauma of Layoffs and Revolutionizing Downsized Organizations.* San Francisco: Jossey-Bass, 1993.

O'Mara, Julie, and Alan Richter. "Global Diversity and Inclusion Benchmarks." 2011. Available at www.QEDConsulting.com.

Pew Hispanic Center, "Statistical Report of the Foreign Born Population in the United States, 2009," Table 2: Population Change by Nativity: 2000 and 2009. Available at http://pewhispanic.org/files/factsheets/foreignborn2009/Table%202.pdf.

Patterson, Kerry, Joseph Grenny, David Maxfield, Ron McMillan, and Al Switzlet. *Influencer: The Power to Change Anything.* New York: McGraw-Hill, 2008.

Pellet, Lizz. *Cultural Fit Factor: Creating an Employment Brand That Attracts, Retains, and Repels the Right Employees.* Alexandria, VA: Society for Human Resource Management, 2009.

"Really Loving Your Neighbor," *The Economist,* March 15, 2007, 66. Available at www.economist.com/node/8859092.

Richter, Alan. "Global Diversity and Multicultural Competence" (online course). 2009. Available at www.swissvbs.com.

Rosinski, Phillipe. *Coaching Across Cultures: New Tools for Leveraging National, Corporate, and Professional Differences.* Boston: Nicholas Brealey, 2003.

Ryan, James. *Inclusive Leadership*. San Francisco: Jossey-Bass, 2005.

Schramm, Jennifer. *Workplace Trends and Forecasting: An Overview of the Findings of the Latest SHRM Workplace Forecast*. Workplace Visions, no. 3. Alexandria, VA: Society of Human Resource Management, 2008.

Simons, George F. *EuroDiversity: A Business Guide to Managing Difference*. Woburn, MA: Elsevier Science, 2002.

Society for Human Resource Management. "Introduction to the Human Resource Discipline of Diversity." Available at www.shrm.org/hrdisciplines/Diversity/Pages/DiversityIntro.aspx.

Stewart, Edward C., and Milton J. Bennett. *American Cultural Patterns: A Cross-Cultural Perspective*. rev. ed. Yarmouth, ME: Intercultural Press, 1991.

Stringer, Donna M., and Patricia A. Cassiday. *52 Activities for Exploring Values Differences*. Yarmouth, ME: Nicholas Brealey, 2003.

Sussman, Lyle. "Prejudice and Behavioral Archetypes: A New Model for Cultural-Diversity Training." *Business Communication Quarterly* 60, no. 1 (March 1997): 7-18.

Tapia, Andrés T. *The Inclusion Paradox: The Obama Era and the Transformation of Global Diversity*. Lincolnshire, IL: Hewitt Associates, 2009.

Thomas, David A., and Robin J. Ely. "Making Differences Matter: A New Paradigm for Managing Diversity." *Harvard Business Review* 74, no. 5 (September-October 1996): 79-90.

Triandis, Harry C. *Individualism & Collectivism*. Boulder, CO: Westview Press, 1995.

Trompenaars, Fons, and Hampden-Turner, Charles. *Riding the Waves of Culture: Understanding Cultural Diversity in Global Business*. 2nd ed. New York: McGraw-Hill, 1994.

Tylor, Edward. *Primitive Culture*. New York: J. P. Putnam, 1920. First published 1871.

UNESCO. *World Culture Report* 2000. Paris: UNESCO, 2000.

U.S. Census Bureau. Language Use in the United States: 2007, American Community Survey Reports (issued April 2010). By Hyon B. Shin and Robert A. Kominski. U.S. Department of Commerce. Available at www.census.gov/hhes/socdemo/language.

United States Bureau of Labor Statistics. "Labor Force Projects by Age." Available at www.bls.gov/spotlight/2011/women/data.htm#ilc_labor_force.

"Occupational Outlook Handbook, 2010-11 Edition." Available at www.bls.gov/oco/oco2003.htm#labor%20force.

United States Department of Homeland Security. Task Force for New Americans. *Building an Americanization Movement for the Twenty-first Century: A Report to the President of the United States from the Task Force on New Americans.* Washington, DC: U.S. Government Printing Office, 2008. Available at www.uscis.gov/files/nativedocuments/M-708. pdf.

United States Equal Employment Opportunity Commission. "Charge Statistics FY 1997 Through FY 2010." http://www.eeoc.gov/eeoc/statistics/enforcement/charges.cfm.

Wall Street Journal, The, "Leadership—The Journal Report," November 14, 2005.

Ward, Colleen. "Psychological Theories of Culture Contact and their Implications for Training and Interventions," In *Handbook of Intercultural Training.* 3rd ed. Edited by Daniel Landis, Janet M. Bennett, and Milton J. Bennett, 185-216. Thousand Oaks, CA: Sage, 2004.

Wells, Susan J. "Layoff Aftermath: Learn How to Minimize the Aftereffects of Layoffs." *HR Magazine,* November 2008.

Whitelaw, Kevin. "Diversity Efforts Uneven in U.S. Companies." National Public Radio. January 11, 2010. Available at www.npr.org/templates/story/story.php?storyId=122329851.

Endnotes

Chapter 1

[1] *Global Diversity.*
[2] *Global Diversity,* 3.
[3] Lewis, *Cultural Imperative,* 115-120.
[4] SHRM, "Introduction to the Human Resource Discipline of Diversity."
[5] Wall Street Journal, The, *Leadership—The Journal Report,* November 14, 2005.

Chapter 2

[1] U.S. Bureau of Labor Statistics, "Labor Force Projects by Age." Future projections also point to the fact that more women in the workforce will be older (see the table below).
[2] U.S. Bureau of Labor Statistics, "Occupational Outlook Handbook, 2010-2011 Edition."
[3] Whitelaw, "Diversity Efforts."
[4] IBM, "Diversity 3.0™." Reprint Courtesy of International Business Machines Corporation, © International Business Machines Corporation.

5 Frankel, "What Does Management Reveal about Global Diversity Management?"

6 U.S. Equal Employment Opportunity Commission, "Charge Statistics."

7 Adler, *International Dimensions of Organizational Behavior*, 16-20.

8 Pellet, *Cultural Fit Factor*.

9 Ward, "Psychological Theories of Culture Contact and their Implications for Training and Interventions."

10 Laroche and Rocherford, *Recruiting, Retaining and Promoting*.

11 Pew Hispanic Center, "Statistical Report of the Foreign Born Population in the United States, 2009," Table 2: Population Change by Nativity: 2000 and 2009.

12 U.S. Bureau of Labor Statistics. "Occupational Outlook Handbook, 2010-2011 Edition." Chart 2

13 Mor Barak, *Managing Diversity*.

14 For an understanding of the early years of diversity practice, see the works of R. Roosevelt Thomas, in particular, *Beyond Race and Gender* (1991) and *Redefining Diversity* (1996).

15 Grove and Hallowell, "Globalizing Diversity"; Stewart and Bennett, *American Cultural Patterns*.

16 McKinsey & Company, *The War for Talent*.

Chapter 3

1 In his book *The World Is Flat: A Brief History of the Twenty-First Century*, Thomas L. Friedman uses a metaphor for viewing the world as a *level playing field* in terms of commerce, where all competitors have an equal opportunity. He argues that globalized trade, outsourcing, supply-chaining, and political forces have changed the world permanently, for both better and worse. He also argues that the pace of globalization is quickening and will continue to have a growing impact on business organization and practice.

2 "The United States is a good example of the disconnect between social inclusion and other types of Inclusion; it ranks a relatively 25th for social inclusion but first for workplace Inclusion. This can be explained by the strong influence of individuals' religious beliefs on politics, tension between religious groups and low public spending on education," comments the authors of *Global Diversity*, 53.

³ Schramm, *Workplace Trends and Forecasting*, 5.

⁴ Tapia, *The Inclusion Paradox*, 67-68: "As U.S.-based multinationals begin planting the diversity flag in their operation outside the United States, they run into the risk of inadvertently — and somewhat ironically — dismissing alternative interpretations of diversity. While there's good reason to celebrate global diversity push by American multinationals, many of which have strong diversity records in the United States, there are pitfalls that could undermine the successful globalization of diversity and inclusion, if left unchecked."

⁵ As intercultural and HR experts, we started to modify and redesign the content and formats of existing programs — first by fits and starts, then by "connecting the dots" both for pre-global and global companies, more and more conscientiously, as our concept and appropriate methodologies took shape. Along the way, in order to meet the needs of today's companies and busy people, we designed all our programs to be delivered in a format of choice: in instructor-led classroom, in virtual classroom (webcast), or as combination of the two. We also started providing train-the-trainer and trainer-certification programs for diversity development, offering the practical recommendations and tools that make diversity and inclusion work. The diversity leaders were interested in changing their learning platforms — and that led us to seek condensed information with the compatible content in the programs initially designed as solid full-day workshops and as half-day or even lunchtime sessions. The series of "bite size" trainings brought more people to diversity audiences — and this is what the diversity managers were after: they wanted diversity to stay alive, vibrant, popular, and spoken about and to be sought after. They wanted it to have content and format vitality and relevance. Transformation Diversity began to emerge in this process, and it began to fit like a glove.

⁶ The need to advance further diversity development was strongly advocated by Carol Hymowitz who said that "As companies do more and more around the world, diversity isn't simply a matter of what is fair or good public relations. It's a business imperative... A wide swath of corporations, however, don't yet realize that." – See: Hymowitz, *The New Diversity*, R1.

⁷ Babcock, "Survey," Survey of Novations.

[8] A *business case,* as simply defined in Wikipedia, captures the reasoning for initiating a project or task. It is presented in a well-structured written document but also sometimes comes as a short verbal argument or presentation. The logic of the business case is that, whatever the resources such as money or efforts are consumed, they should be in support of a specific business need.

[9] *Global Diversity,* 13-16.

[10] In addition to "increasing internal efficiency" (scoring 53 percent) other business rationales for Diversity-related initiatives, according to survey respondents, include: "a matter of fairness and morality (47 percent), "tapping new talent" (43 percent), "need to be mindful of customers/suppliers" (42 percent), and "complying with equal opportunity laws" (38 percent) – see *Global Diversity,* 16.

[11] Source: *Cumulative Gallup Workplace Studies:* Business Case for Diversity with Inclusion.

[12] One bright example of how positively Inclusion initiatives, employee engagement and creative ideas enhance the bottom line of companies can be seen in development of the new Pepsi-Cola products; at Pepsi, "The goal is an inclusive culture where employees feel free to express their views, even if those are sometimes negative or involve confronting top executives" – and this breeds success. After: Hymowitz, *The New Diversity,* R2.

[13] "The survey confirms that the main barrier to Diversity and Inclusion is cultural resistance within the company itself. Nearly half (46 percent) of respondents say the task of changing HR practices and policies to encourage Diversity is either "somewhat difficult" or "very difficult." Only 18 percent rate the task as either "very easy" or "somewhat easy" (Chart 15, *Global Diversity,* 17)

[14] *Global Diversity,* 16.

[15] *Global Diversity.*

[16] Johansson, *Medici Effect.*

[17] On the quantitative side, nevertheless, Edward E. Hubbard, author of *How to Calculate Diversity Return on Investment* (1999), explains that the way to calculate a correlation is grounded in some theory and explained in detail. This method was not practiced long in the field for some reason, maybe because it takes a lot of effort and money to keep track of and register all necessary data in order to come up with proper quantitative correlation.

[18] Thomas and Ely, "Making Differences Matter," 79-90.

[19] "Scandinavia, North America and Western Europe have the best regional performance for Diversity and Inclusion ... This does not mean that Scandinavian, European or North American countries have fulfilled their potential for Diversity and Inclusion — the best regional score is still only 70 out of 100, and the world score of 52 out of 100 suggests that much work is left to be done on Diversity and Inclusion globally" — see *Global Diversity*, 51. More specifically, on Global Diversity readiness Canada scores 70.1 while the U.S. scores 61.5 — see *Global Diversity*, 19.

[20] Lackey, "Expert."

[21] *Global Diversity*, 14.

[22] As Wells, *Layoff Aftermath*, 38, points out, "When layoffs hit the workplace, the pink-slipped aren't the only victims." The recommended treatment to layoff-survivor sickness is the practices that foster so-called "job-embeddedness" or attachment/inclusion, serving as buffer — which is succinctly described in Wells, *Layoff Aftermath*, 39-41.

[23] Noer, *Healing the Wounds*.

[24] Wells, "Layoff Aftermath"; Noer, *Healing the Wounds*.

[25] Simons, *EuroDiversity*.

[26] Ryan, *Inclusive Leadership*; Hollander, *Inclusive Leadership: The Essential Leader-Follower*.

[27] Huffington, "Year of Hope 2.0," 42.

[28] Lewis, *Cross-Cultural Communication*.

[29] Bartz, "Leadership in the Information Age," 128.

[30] Kwintessential.

[31] "Definition of Intercultural Competence." Suggested by the staff at Universität des Saarlandes.

[32] "Definition of Intercultural Competence." Contributed by Alvino E. Fantini, Ph.D., School for International Training, Brattleboro, Vermont.

[33] "Definition of Intercultural Competence." Suggested by Anna Schmid, UBS AG, Financial Services Group, Zürich.

Chapter 4

[1] Briscoe, Schuler, and Claus, *International Human Resources Management*, Chapter 6.

[2] A further explanation of the history of cultural research may be helpful. More than a century ago, social scientists began to study the matter of culture and to offer definitions of this complex subject. Each of their efforts continued to expose deeper levels of understanding of what constitutes culture and what defines it. The earliest definition offered in the nineteenth century by Edward Tylor in *Primitive Culture* (1871) described culture as "the complex whole . . . of capabilities and habits acquired by man as a member of society." By the mid-twentieth century, definitions began to go beyond observable phenomena and patterning to incorporate an understanding of social psychology. Ideas, beliefs, and values were now part of the understanding of what shaped people's capabilities and habits. The work of the anthropologists Kluckhorn and Strodbeck (1961), in particular, identified a limited number of value-based questions, to which every society or group of individuals, historical and present, has responded. These questions deal with matters of human relationships, time, human activity, human nature, and nature itself. Consequently, over time, cultural research has identified a large number of general and specific orientations or measurable tendencies transmitted through groups of individuals, using a value basis. This brief history is important in understanding the development of value-based methodologies used by more recent social scientists such as Geert Hofstede (1991, 1997, and 2010) and Fons Trompenaars and Charles Hampden-Turner (1994) to explore corporate organizations as cultural entities. They and others produced a body of knowledge consisting of a number of cultural constructs (or dimensions) now used widely in intercultural studies and management. There are many resources available for the interested reader to pursue the specifics of these studies.

[3] Hofstede, *Cultures and Organizations*.

[4] Tapia, *The Inclusion Paradox*, 3.

[5] Adler, *International Dimensions of Organizational Behavior*, 77.

[6] Triandis, *Individualism & Collectivism*, 13.

[7] Hofstede, *Cultures and Organizations, 92–96*.

[8] Martine Abdallah-Pretceille, "Interculturalism as a Paradigm for Thinking about Diversity."

[9] U.S. Department of Homeland Security, Task Force for New Americans, *Building an Americanization Movement*.

[10] Lewis, *Cultural Imperative.*

[11] Friedman, *The Lexus and the Olive Tree.*

[12] Simons, *EuroDiversity.*

[13] UNESCO, *World Culture Report 2000.*

[14] Grove and Hallowell, "Globalizing Diversity."

[15] Trompenaars and Hamden-Turner, *Riding the Waves of Culture.*

[16] Bennett and Bennett, "Developing Intercultural Sensitivity: An Integrative Approach to Global and Domestic Diversity," 147-165.

[17] O'Mara and Richter, "Global Diversity and Inclusion Bookmarks."

[18] Hyun, *Breaking the Bamboo Ceiling.*

Chapter 5

[1] Sussman, "Predjudice and Behavioral Archetypes."

[2] Garreau, *Nine Nations of North America*, 1-13.

[3] Gallup, "Americans See U.S. as Exceptional; 37% Doubt Obama Does."

[4] Stringer and Cassiday, *52 Activities.*

[5] Patterson et al., *Influencer.*

[6] Himsel, *Leadership Sopranos Style*, 167-184.

[7] Mayer, *Collaborative Competition™.*

[8] Leki, "Reality Therapy for Intercultural Training," 12.

[9] Black et. al., *Globalizing People through International Assignments.*

[10] Hampden-Turner and Trompenaars, *Building Cross-Cultural Competence.*

[11] Lewis, *Cross-Cultural Communication.*

[12] The ACROSS© Model, based on intercultural research coupled with practical training and designed by Eric J. Kruger, has seventy-two cultural variables addressing much more than national culture. It was tested in over 2,000 real-life training and executive coaching sessions and reviewed by a multinational panel of intercultural professionals. *EXPERT MS Inc.* has exclusive world rights to the ACROSS© Model which is published for the first time.

[13] *US Census Bureau*, 8-9: as of 2007 population percent of those who speak a language other than English at home is 19.7 for the United States. Specifically, "the percentage of people who spoke a language other than English at home varied substantially across states; just 2 percent of West Virginians 5 years old and over reported speaking a language other than English at home, while

43 percent of people in California reported the same. Moreover, Figure 3 shows that relatively high levels of other language speakers were common in the Southwest and in the larger immigrant gateway states of the East, such as New York, New Jersey, and Florida. With the exception of Illinois, relatively lower levels of foreign-language speakers prevail in most of the Midwest and in the South."

14 Boggs, "E-Learning Benefits"; Kruse and Keil, *Technology-Based Training*.

15 Boggs, "E-Learning Benefits."

16 Groen and Parrs, "Bringing Cross-Cultural Communication," 3-7.

17 Richter, "Global Diversity and Multicultural Competence."

18 Mayer, *Collaborative Competition*™, 227-244.

19 *Really Loving Your Neighbor*, 66: "Mr Pittinsky's hope is to turn the conventional wisdom of "conflict studies" and "race relations" upside down. There is a huge body of knowledge, he says, on prejudice against races or other categories. What he wants to promote, both as a scholarly tool and policy goal, is "allophilia"—liking for other groups—and the behaviour it inspires. "So much research aims to understand racist and xenophobic attitudes, so much policy aims to counter such attitudes—but people neglect to look at positive attitudes to other groups," says Mr Pittinsky, a professor at Harvard's Centre for Public Leadership. He believes that "allophilia" is a measurable state of mind with hard consequences. For example, the attitude of an American voter towards immigration is determined less accurately by party affiliation or social and economic status than by the degree to which he or she simply likes Latinos. And people's choices in charitable giving, study, voluntary work and travel are guided, not surprisingly, by the sort of groups that make them feel good."

Appendix A

1 This summary also includes details provided by Milton Bennett in a separate document available at www.library.wisc.edu/edvrc/docs/public/pdfs/SEEDReadings/intCulSens.pdf.

2 Bennett and Bennett, "Developing Intercultural Sensitivity," 157.

Index

Acknowledgements

First, we are deeply blessed to have the love and support of our respective families, and we are grateful for their presence, comfort, support, and encouragement throughout the process of writing this book.

Here we want to acknowledge those who played a part either in discussing the Transformational Diversity approach at the time when it was still budding, or in shaping the logistics of the book:

To Dr. George F. Simons, creator of Diversophy®, an intercultural and diversity professional and outstanding thinker, whose judgment and generous advice are without peer; he advised us in the early pioneering stage of the book and helped to express Transformational Diversity vision as a more clear-cut, comprehensive, and applicable approach and practice;

To Peter W. Hayward, founder and Senior Partner of Expanding Horizons International and a prominent interculturalist, who read the first version of the book and provided his valuable remarks and support at that early stage, much appreciated;

To Cecelia Holloway, Managing Director of Diversity and Inclusion, Americas, at UBS Investment Bank, whose unmatched creativity, dedication to Diversity-for-the-people, and enthusiasm about Transformational Diversity adding to her company's bottom line proved very stimulating for us in the past three years. Specifically, while working with Ci Ci on customizing our programs for UBS every time the resulting program had a distant resemblance to the original prototype, and it is from here that the notion of Action Archetypes took shape;

To Philip Berry, former Vice President of Global Workplace Initiatives at Colgate, now President of Philip Berry Associates LLC, who never let us forget that the pragmatic, practical approach to both domestic and global Diversity should always be at the forefront; this influenced our thinking in the direction of spearheading Transformational Diversity to contribute more to the bottom line;

To Dr. Mitra Chappell, now Diversity & Inclusion Director of Kellogg Company, the discussion with whom on one hot summer day in New York is the lesson well taken: it was then that the critical difference between Diversity and Inclusion became very clear to us: Diversity is a State of Mind and Inclusion is Action. It was also quick-thinking Mitra who was the first to diagnose that Transformational Diversity is a vision, not simply a concept;

To Robert S. Nadel, former President of HR-New York and President of Nadel Consulting Group Inc., for his unwavering support of all endeavors new and also for making a leap of faith and encouraging further work on our book at its initial stage;

To Stephanie Quappe, Diversity Manager at Deloitte Touche Tohmatsu Limited, whose comprehensive advice was a great help in polishing the final version of our book: as a former colleague in facilitating programs for intercultural skill-building in global teams, she readily shared her passion and knowledge. Some of her experiences in developing programs for new immigrants, such as herself, made their way into breaking new ground in Deloitte's Diversity activities and into her recommendations regarding our book. In particular, Stephanie was also instrumental in advising us to put final touches on the Transformational Diversity Action Archetype V, Women World Wide;

To Walter Hurdle, Director of Diversity at Merck, who — over five years ago — was the first to appreciate the "America the Diverse" program and remarked that Diversity, like charity, should start at home, so one could set in motion the U.S. diversity first, and based on that proceed to all things global. We kept it in mind when making "America the Diverse" Action Archetype a basic building block on the way to global diversity;

To Susan Farwell and Ariel Boverman, who has managed International Special Interest Group of HR/NY for many years now, for organizing a joint session of International and Diversity groups of Human Resources-New York in November of 2008. It was there that Transformational Diversity "went public" — we could present the budding Transformational Diversity approach and discuss it with all interested professionals; that was a turning point in the Transformational Diversity vision/concept development;

To others who assisted us — without their direct knowledge — but because of what we learned from working with them — such as colleagues and friends involved in managing some of the earliest Global Diversity initiatives at Deloitte, especially Jim Wall, Managing Director of Talent Management, along with Alan Richter and Willa Hallowell, true professionals, passionate in all matters of Diversity and intercultural learning;

To our students of Cross-Cultural Education, we are grateful for their inspiration. They are eager to learn how to build bridges to manage intercultural differences and are undaunted in learning that Inclusion is hard work, and because of this they give us hope for a better world full of cooperation and less conflict;

Mostly, we are grateful to each other: for intellectual stimulus all the way, from inception to completion of this book. Coming from some very different walks of life and wearing different cultural makeup, we were able to come to deeply understanding each other, taming our egos, and learning to contribute to and enrich our mutual thinking process.

About the Authors

Fiona Citkin, Ph.D., is a founder and Managing Director of Expert MS Inc., an international consulting firm specializing in business-aligned Intercultural Business Competencies and Transformational Diversity setup and implementation. Fiona's experiences as a professional diversi-culturalist, linguist, and intercultural educator include a career in academia and being a Fulbright Scholar in Cross-Cultural and Translation Studies, as well as a Director at Berlitz and FGI. A keen observer of the new trends in her area of competence, active in SIETAR-USA, SIETAR-Metro New York, Human Resources-New York, and SHRM, a Board member of Global E-Learning and Associate Member of IMI (American University), she is also an accomplished facilitator who previously authored a book along with many research articles. She can be reached at fiona.citkin@expertms.com.

Lynda Spielman, Ph.D., GPHR, is now a global HR consultant and educator on many global workforce issues and is especially experienced in implementing cultural diversity in business practices. She is retired from Deloitte Touche Tohmatsu, where she directed both global mobility programs and the organization's global strategy on

Multiculturalism and Inclusion. She is also an Adjunct Assistant Professor in Intercultural Education at New York University and in International Human Resources at NYIT. Lynda has been active in the HR community as a representative to the International Personnel Association, a member of the Berlitz Advisory Board, Chair of the HR group for the British American Business Institute, and as a member/presenter for HRNY and local SHRM programs. She can be reached at lyndaspielman@aol.com.

Additional SHRM-Published Books

Business-Focused HR: 11 Processes to Drive Results
By Scott P. Mondore, Shane S. Douthitt, and Marisa A. Carson

Business Literacy Survival Guide for HR Professionals
By Regan W. Garey

The Chief HR Officer: Defining the New Role of Human Resource Leaders
By Patrick M. Wright, John W. Boudreau, David A. Pace, Elizabeth "Libby" Sartain, Paul McKinnon, and Richard L. Antoine

The Cultural Fit Factor: Creating an Employment Brand That Attracts, Retains, and Repels the Right Employees
By Lizz Pellet

The Essential Guide to Federal Employment Laws
By Lisa Guerin and Amy DelPo

The Essential Guide to Workplace Investigations: How to Handle Employee Complaints & Problems
By Lisa Guerin

From Hello to Goodbye: Proactive Tips for Maintaining Positive Employee Relations
By Christine V. Walters

Got a Minute? The 9 Lessons Every HR Professional Must Learn to Be Successful
By Dale J. Dwyer and Sheri A. Caldwell

HR Competencies: Mastery at the Intersection of People and Business
By Dave Ulrich, Wayne Brockbank, Dani Johnson, Kurt Sandholtz, and Jon Younger

Human Resource Essentials: Your Guide to Starting and Running the HR Function
By Lin Grensing-Pophal

Proving the Value of HR: How and Why to Measure ROI
By Jack J. Phillips and Patricia Pulliam Phillips

Stop Bullying at Work: Strategies and Tools for HR and Legal Professionals
By Teresa A. Daniel

For a comprehensive list, please visit: www.shrm.org/Publications/Books/Pages/default.aspx.